UNMASKED

Spirit Flares

Joanna Francis

**KO
RA**

**K O R A
P R E S S**

UNMASKED

Spirit Flares

*A collection of poems and cameo writings,
first published in newsletters, magazines
or books*

Joanna Francis

By the same author:

Learn How to Read a Palm
The Theatre of the Tarot
In-Formation: Moments of Realization
In-Tuition: Moments of Awakening
In-Sight: Moments of Being
Dear Gabriel: Letters From a Trainee Angel
Rainbow Woman: How to fulfill the 7 ages of your life
The I Ching for Women

I dedicate this book to my dear companions who share this adventure called life with optimism and a hope for something better, and specially to my friend and life partner, David Francis, who is always there ready to share a new insight and new inspiration.

CONTENTS:

POEM POT POURI p. 13

White-White-White
The Drum
To Dare
Seven Expressions of Honor
Mr. Midnight
A Detection Process
A New Endeavor
On the Way to Croton
Constancy
Request
Other Lives
The Mission
Defiance
Change
Serenity
May I Be Like a Child
I'm in a Play
Choice

REMINDERS TO ME p.29

A Mark of Respect
Chance
The Unlimited Me
The Long Term View
God's Needs
A Time to Heal
A Touch
The Open Bird Cage
A Surprise
Awake
Asleep
Call-over
Questions
The Silence of the Sound
Praise to the Law of Duality

The Rainbow Journey
An Essence Speaks
My Religion
Increase in Perception

QUALITIES p. 45

Introduction
Forgiveness
Leadership
Trust
Generosity
Understanding
Sublimation
Hospitality
Art
Peace
Freedom
Ora
Acceptance and Rejection
The Vision
Qualities Meditation

CREATION GIVES, THE HUMAN RESPONDS p. 63

A One Act Play

EARTH POEMS p. 67

Childhood
(The Planet Speaks)
The Planet's Lament
(Earth Day)
The Colors of Fall
Mother of Renewal
The Summer Flower
The River
I Must Be Like the Water
Thank You

WRITINGS FROM THE DESERT p. 77

Com-Passion—the many ways of giving
A Call-over – Asking for Warmth
Many Warmths
Give
Farewell to the Desert

CHILD'S PLAY p. 83

Musings About Life, the World and Me

LIGHTER FARE p. 89

The Bread Maker
Two Clocks
A Voice
A Good Deed
The Pool—A Lament
A Problem

GENDER WRITINGS p. 95

Women Carrying Water
Hope
Salute the Gentleman
Redefining Femininity
The 9 Gifts and the 10 Blessings
My Life as a Woman
(A Monologue)

CAMEO WRITINGS p. 111

On Waiting
Permission
The Language Soliloquy
(A Lament)
Fear
To My Soul and to Me

STORIES FROM THE PAST p. 123

Experience of a London Bombing
Jadwiga
Knowing the Name of the Enemy

IN PURSUIT OF DEVELOPMENT p. 133

Red and White Revival
Value
What Makes Something Valuable
The Value of Food
Clairvoyance
Every Moment Counts
Outside the Churcch
So Many
Aging
Change

GOD'S DESIGNERS SERIES p. 147

Introduction
The Human
The Voice
Feet
The Eyes
The Ear
The Blood
A Tree

A MIXED BAG p. 163

Comparison
Salad
A Look at Human and World History
(The Two Views)
Compassion
Meditation
Presents or presence?
The Greatest Present of All
Speaking of Tongues

The New Year
The Planet of Birds
A Letter to My Body
The Three Trains
The Spring
The Fence's Lament
Your Face
Aging
To Think It Is to Create It
or Your Reality and You
Honesty
Mint Will Grow in the Garden
A Thought About Honor
Likes and Dislikes
Meditation About Likes and Dislikes
Entities yet Unknown
It Has Been so Long
What I Want
The Partnership
Out of the Dark
Meditation
Why Is the Human on Earth?
Living with Grace
The Trail of Tears
The Wand of Youth and the Dawn of Life
When I Die
When I Die 2

STREETS OF THE MIND p. 215

Introduction
Boa Street
Lo Street
Co Street
Pa Street
La Street
Mo and Be Street
Fa Street

Poem Pot Pouri

White—White—White

From the distance of time
From the depth of Topeth
Comes the white—
the unbiased, unwritten, impartial plasma
Within which everything can happen.
And does and will and did.

It emerges clean and pure, ready to assist and be used.
It emits a pulse—tick, tock, tick, tock
And in the pauses between the two
you can hear the silence
Where lives the yet unwritten symphony.

From the white emerge all colors
Coloring the world, with shades and hues
And from the radiance of the soul
The red, the blue, the green and the yellow appear.
Four sentinels, four realizations, four appearances,
Adding flavor, interpretation and new potential
To the cleanliness of the yet unwritten white.

He wit, with E, it hew.
The white allows usage.
The newly formed human is given a soul and the time
within which to instruct it,
Flavor it and establish a working relationship with it.

Mercilessly it moves on—
Emit—time—it/me
It waits for no one but allows everything.
In time or out of time, on time or with time to spare—
Don't kill time, but save time
Your most precious gift is time.

It moves on, like a pendulum that winds down
until the final moments are spent.
Chronos, old father time,
runs away from you like a young child
in his white winged sneakers.

The white marks a new beginning, a rite of passage—
A christening gown, a first communion,
a wedding dress, a funeral shroud.
It moves in cycles, anti-clockwise,
in harmony with the planet and its seasons.
Re-emerging fresh and new again, again and again.

With white there is a rhythm,
ancient and young at the same time;
Primordial and eternal.
Tick, tock; tick, tock.
It reminds us of our mortality, our renewal
and of the promise of the resurrection,
Whatever that might mean for thee.

The Drum

The drum beats to the rhythm of the heart and
the heart beats to the rhythm of the drum.
Both beat in harmony with the Earth and all three
respond to the pulse of Creation,
As it awakens, invigorates, accompanies, taunts,
encourages and challenges all life on Earth.

All life is rhythm and it ebbs and flows,
rises and abates in cycles,
Moving forever forward, like a river flowing
downstream through rapids and eddies,
Over waterfalls and weirs;
on and on the dance continues.

Always have people moved and swayed—
danced to the rhythm of the land
As it pulsates and throbs
and radiates to its own unique beat.
Slow in the lowlands, faster in the mountains,
melodic in the hills, monotonously in the plains...
Haunting in the forest, playful in the fields,
longing by the sea, determined in the steppes...
The dance continues.

To Dare

Don't worry who you are my lady fair
That your face is plain or you don't like your hair
It is so much more important
to have patience and care
And that you want to work
to make life on Earth more fair.
Application and hope,
and the fact that you dare
Go out on a limb
with your wings and your prayer.

Seven Expressions of Honor

I honor my existence, it is a platform for all
I honor my gender, it makes me walk tall
I honor the men, the other side of God's face
I honor what can happen within an embrace
I honor the experience that life showers upon me
I honor the planet—the sky, land and sea
I honor it all for as long as I live
And am able to learn, to live and to give.

Mr. Midnight

I

He walks through the town
When everyone's asleep
His footsteps echo through the street
He knows that no one's watching him.

II

Mr. Midnight carries a bag full of magic
that no one else wants.
He takes it back where he belongs
to the land where magic abounds.

III

I know him from my dreams
and wait for him night after night.
But just as he is about to come down the street
my eyes close and I fall asleep.

A Detection Process

Play for me the music, all that is the best
Show me the art, open up the treasure chest
Poetry and literature, read to me as well
Let me hear the story that they have to tell.

I will look and listen, with attention and care
So that I may understand what is not yet there.

A New Endeavor

*The following writing was inspired by witnessing a new endeavor
and a new vision being born, supported by a team of like-minded
individuals.*

Caught between elation and a tear
The vision seems so far and yet so near
To touch it, feel it, know that it exists
Is that enough? the thought persists.

Can I remember, can I make a space
To integrate with quite a different pace?
To carry the vision like a torch up high?
So that it can be more than a passing sigh?

On the Way to Croton

On the way to Croton
Something important needs to be thought of,
Something important needs to be said.
Why does the journey back seem so much shorter?
Has someone sneaked in and folded part of the road up
and taken it away in the meantime
Or is it only shorter in my head?

If so, then I am rich beyond measure
For I have found a way to prolong my existence,
to prolong each and every journey that I make
I have managed with stubborn insistence
To wrestle this secret from the road that I take:

"Always be sure to make only outward journeys
Only first time experiences
First time encounters,
see everything as new every day
And the journey will be long,
the life full and the dealings rich."
(I know this bit doesn't rhyme, but it needed to be said
in these words. I guess the road is no poet.)

"Conversely, when in a hurry, decide this is known
Make it a repeat experience and it won't be long,
Like a favorite refrain in a favorite song.

"For however long or short you want it to be,
There is a hand that writes your destiny
The reasons, the purpose, the vision, the aim
Will determine what is new
and what is the same again, again and again."

The poem opposite was written after a morning meditation conducted in quiet solitude on the banks of the Westchester reservoir.

Constancy

Constancy allows something real to build and grow
Its roots may be small, but the heart will know
With steadfastness and regularity shall I proceed
To collect qualities and essences according to need.

So never mind the repetition
if you want your vision to reach the sky
For how long did it take you to learn to walk
from the moment of your first try?

Request

Please wait until I pass this mental gate
Do me the honor to patiently wait
Let me bind words to feelings and set them free
So you and I both can understand
what is troubling me.

Bear with me a moment and then I will receive
All you want to say and what you believe
Then I will listen and take time to parry
But now is my turn, so I ask you to tarry.

Two ears, one mouth the Creator has made
For each one of us to use and to be not afraid
Listen, listen, say; listen, listen, say
Learn to respond in the Creational way.

Other Lives

My mind goes back to months before my birth
The decision made—"This spirit goes back to Earth."
And then the search for a family that would take me in
Where my new life adventure would begin.

Did I choose where I would first appear?
Did I select my human Mom and Dad?
Was it so that I might better challenge fear?
And discover what is good and what is bad?

Was it a debt that still remained unpaid?
Reaching out from my history's store?
Or was it the result of the fact that I had prayed
And asked that in this life I might discover more?

And when the time comes to leave this earthly plane
And all that could be said and done is done
Will I hope to have another chance
to come back here again?
Or will I be settled to all that I had lost and won?

So when I go I have but one wish, one hope, one desire
That there will be no regrets left and no fear
So I can face the future with an inner fire
To offer service as life's next stage draws near.

The Mission

The Mission is to not miss the ions
that are already there
To provide anchorage for the spirits of the air,
The water and the earth, and the fire, too
The Spectrum, Green, Yellow, Red, White and Blue.

Not to forget the Silver and the Gold,
And all fine qualities, both new and old;
Everything fine that is looking for roots
That can help in development,
from our heads to our boots.

Creating an ecology, a template, a dome
That high unseen worlds would want to call home
A place of refinement, unique on planet Earth
Where we can commune with the spirit,
and to new templates give birth.

A constant standard, a bit like a well,
Where something spiritual can come and can dwell.
Where or when that will be, no one can tell
But we have all been influenced, cast under its spell.

So to take a step back—we would need to be fit
To give It the room, to listen to It.
So It can lead, heal and whisper in our ear
What is next needed and why we are here.

So in short—the mission is for unification
A new type of community, a new template nation
In harmony with Earth, the people, the fizz,
So we can move into the future
and be open to the next WHAT IS.

Defiance

I am the spirit of defiance
And I invite you to the dance.
Defy—sky high,
Defy—sky high.

Born into a family
Born onto a place
Defined too early
Is the story of the human race.

I am the spirit of defiance
And I invite you to the dance.
Defy—sky high,
Defy—sky high.

Then taught the views
Accepted by the group
Ready prepared news,
Here's the latest scoop.

I am the spirit of defiance
And I invite you to the dance.
Defy—sky high,
Defy—sky high.

"Think for yourself,"
Your mentors will cry.
But only if the thinking
With their views does comply.

I am the spirit of defiance
And I invite you to the dance.
Defy—sky high,
Defy—sky high.

You are given the book,
The computer, the mouse
You can discover and look
All round the world,
without leaving the house.

I am the spirit of defiance
And I invite you to the dance.
Defy—sky high,
Defy—sky high.

If you want to take part
In the leadership plan
You must follow the party
You must be a man.

I am the spirit of defiance
And I invite you to the dance.
Defy—sky high,
Defy—sky high.

If this poem stirs you,
Ask yourself why.
What is your unique view?
And how much do you try?

I am the spirit of defiance
And I invite you to the dance.
Defy—sky high,
Defy—sky high.

Change

I

"I don't believe in the event,"
said the young branch to the old,
"and although I can feel in my sap it is getting cold,
white fluff falling from heaven? Never!
It is too advanced a concept for my young bark to hold.
My imagination is conservative and not quite so bold,
And I just cannot believe everything I am told."

II

Until the time happened when the frost and snow came
And the young bough bowed its body
under the weight and in shame—
"I must remember next time
that nothing ever remains the same."

Serenity

Do not become attached to any one place
Do not covet the beauty of someone else's face
For you are here for such a short stay
That you need to be ready to go, night or day.

So do your best and make a mark
For you are here for such a short spark.
Do what you love and love what you do
And I will be there to accompany you.

May I Be Like a Child

May I be like a child, always asking why
And always seeing something new
when I look at the sky.
May I remain open, ready to receive
So that with intuition I am able to believe
There is always more to understand and perceive
So let me tire not, let me persevere.

I'm in a Play

I don't know the script, but I'm in a play
In fact I am cast in a leading part
The plot keeps unfolding day by single day
I don't know when it will end,
though I can trace the start.

As I write my life I interact with co-stars and the cast
We improvise as we go along
Our instinct is the prompter; it is accurate and fast
It teaches each our unique song.

The producer is absent but makes herself known
Through feelings and hunches and dreams
She lets me know I am never alone
And that life is always more than it seems.

Choice

You have been given the freedom to choose
To say yes or say no, to win or to lose.
Everything is possible, it's ours to create
What we embody—is it destiny or fate?

Who are you?
Which codings of Creation have you found
To bring into your life
before you go back to the ground?
Will you give service or live for self gain?
Develop your talents, or learn to play the game?

As you move on, what will you become?
Will you have wisdom and brightness
when your time is done?
Are you acquiescent to change and happy to die
To this life and this time, to be able to try
To start over again and develop and change
To go to the stars or come back here again?

Do you think you are part of
something greater than you?
And will you support it in all that you do?
Are you conscious, unconscious, or can you have two?
To know, understand Creation and you?

And where there are two, there will always be three:
A triune of God, Creation and me.

March 5, 2004

Reminders to Me

A Mark of Respect

When I get up in the morning
and my feet reach for the floor
I have a little call-over
that came to me before.
As I straighten out my spine
and ignore the creaks and pain
I think that this is a special gift
and here I am again.
To stand up straight confirms the act
our ancestors did pioneer
And it must have been a struggle then
to persist despite the fear
And so when I stand, I make a mark,
it is a mark from me
To confirm the courage and tenacity
in the effort to be free.

Chance

It is the experience of beast and man
That nothing goes according to plan
There is always new learning, a new way to be,
When confronted with the variant,
like stormy weather at sea.

So when you arrange to perform a task
at twenty to four,
Something unexpected will come to pass
a stranger might knock on your door.
So be always prepared for what you cannot foresee
And be happy to adapt to what wants to be.

The Unlimited Me

Beyond feeling, beyond longing
and beyond the greatest pain
Is a calling that beckons me again and again.
With no history, no description and even no name
It speaks to the part of me that is the same—
Yet to be conquered, printed or tamed.

A void that defies words, ineffable and pure
It will not respond to enticement,
reasoning or lure;
A mystery, a secret, an enigma yet unknown,
It holds the future and the past,
and I am no longer alone.

May 24, 2003

The Long Term View

The magic carpet takes me away
Beyond the minute, the hour, the day
Into a vision of a future time
When my long term view will no longer be mine.

What does Creation want, I ask.
And how does that define my short term task?
Between me and it I see a silver band
That connects me to the future, if I now make a stand.

God's Needs

"What are God's needs?" the old sage asked,
as the acolyte came to the test.
It was time for the young man to become unmasked
And to show both his worst and his best.

"What are God's needs?" the young man again asked
Lifting his brow in surprise.
"I think I have been unfairly tasked,
For how do I begin to surmise?

"My needs are many," he continued to say,
As he searched through the halls of his brain.
"I need food and shelter, and a place to pray,
Companionship and to be able to maintain…"

"Stop!" said the sage, "you don't understand!
Your needs are known and within reach.
The planet provides—the air and the land,
The Host and the spirit all teach.

"But do you listen and do you know?
You are unfinished, potentially great,
On a journey together to the high from the low
With the option to pass through the gate.

"God is your mentor, God is your friend,
God waits for you to excel in your art.
The journey towards God has no beginning or end;
Believe in yourself for a start!"

A Time to Heal

Three in the morning Israeli time
And I still can't get to sleep
Something inside me wants to rejoice
Another part wants to weep.

Three in the morning and a time to dwell
On stories my ancestors longed to tell
These are my family, as I have been told
Departed too early, never to grow old.
Their voices ring with the wisdom of years
Acquired through centuries of sweat, toil and tears.

"There have been many holocausts,"
they try to explain
"Many lives have perished, many more to blame.
A continuous cycle of crime, guilt and accusation
It has not eluded any single nation.
History is stained, it is dirty and scarred;
You can find it in books, no need to look hard.
Everywhere is greed—essences below the line,
Arguments of ownership—'it's not yours, it's mine!'

"But there comes a time
when something else must begin
A third vector presence, which means both sides win.
To rise above the suffering and pain,
To be able to start fresh and begin again.
Just as in the spring
a fresh blade of grass will appear,
So must you evolve and learn to conquer fear.
Now is your time to make your special mark;
The new order starts here;
we are coming out of the dark."

A Touch

Reach out! And as your arm extends
The touch, your touch, it never ends.
A vast cosmology at your fingertips
Connecting brain to eyes and lips.
Is that an angel or a flow of air
That I can sense is moving there?
Trust your hand and you may find
There are others of like mind.

The Open Bird Cage

Open up the bird cage,
Let your bird go free
Enter a renewed stage
of your destiny.

Let it fly, let it fly, let it fly
It will be back by and by.

In your mental birdcage
All your views are stored
Open up a new page
Make some room for more.

This is the hour, this is the day, this is the time,
Connect to the future, throw it a line.

New thoughts are a-waiting
Queuing up outside
Don't be hesitating
Swim against the tide.

Let it free, let it free, let it free
Connect to your destiny!

A Surprise

I look into the sky at night
and wonder—is there anybody there?
And if they are looking out at me,
To what can they compare?

In a galaxy far away
Someone wonders, asking why
But do they measure time by hours
And do they look into the sky?

Do they know where they are going
and do they see what I can see?
Is there war or peace out there
And do they know that I am me?

Is their home a mild place
Or do they have to combat cold?
Have they water, wind and fire?
How old are they when they are old?

Do they breathe and is it air?
Or do they feed a different way?
Have they gold and is it rare?
Do they work and do they pray?

If I strain my ears and listen
I think I hear their voices ring
Someone's calling me to join them
Someone's causing me to sing.

Awake

As I wake up this morning and enter into this day,
I will remember this:

Today is the day I begin. It is for me a fresh start,
a new opportunity and a clean slate.
Give me the strength to see this theater of life
with new eyes.

Grant me the wisdom to use my experience wisely.
Don't let me take this time allotted to me for granted—
I have it but once.
Help me remember that I am the forger of my future
and that I am not alone.

May generosity be my guiding light and today
may I add to my value of kind and Creation.
May I always give to receive, work to earn what I get
and never assume that I am owed anything.
Above all, may I stay clean.

This day may I take one small step towards
my destiny.

So help me Creation, the stars, the sun, the planet,
the unseen friends, me...

Asleep

As I lay myself to sleep, may I think on this:
Another day has passed within which Creation has
displayed its constancy. Let there be continuance.

From this day I will carry forward the good times;
from all the others will I learn what not to do
and how not to be.

This night may sleep replenish my body and energy
invigorate my soul.

May I remember that in giving up control I trust the
gentle healings of Creation's ways. May I remember
that I am part of this great new arising and that every
moment is a precious gift, to be used wisely and with
appreciation.

So help me Creation, the stars, the sun, the planet,
the unseen friends, me...

Call-Over

You be there for each other
And I will be there for you.

Give to me the ability to discern
What is a true need
and what is none of my concern
To take on a tasking I can truly do well
And to speak
when there is something worthwhile to tell.

Let me conserve energy, but expend it when it's due
To help another, or heal, or connect to frequencies new.
Let me not waste what is left of this special time,
May it be of account, may it be sublime!

Questions

Are you King, Queen or Knave?
Are you master or a slave?
Do you control your own fate?
And are you early, on time or late?

The Silence of the Sound

The silence of the sound
Is freedom still unbound
Before the writing of the note,
Before the words leave home of throat.

The silence of the sound
Means something magic is around
Before the tuning of the bass,
A quiet room, a sacred space.

In the silence of the sound
All the dreams and hopes abound.
It can happen, it can come,
Before the beating of the drum.

June 26, 2002

Praise to the Law of Duality

Still up in the middle of the night
Somehow things just don't feel right...
One thing is certain—there is come and go,
So this will also pass, I know.

Good times, bad times, each a gift,
Appreciation comes with two...
Out of struggle new thoughts lift;
Each day life is born anew.

Tomorrow is another day,
A new beginning and a new way.
Look into the sky my friend
The universe, it has no end.

The Rainbow Journey

RED (0-11)
The energy of childhood is red—
vibrant and warm
Full of learning, discovery,
every day is a storm.
In your hunger to find out
you keep striving to know
And your appearance keeps changing
as you continue to grow.

ORANGE (12-22)
Then enters orange, the signal comes next
That teaches you to appreciate
the joys and angst of sex.
Becoming an adult can cause you to feel
That being all grown up is soberingly real.
You try out new things, some work and some fun,
First decisions are made
as to who you want to become.

YELLOW (23-33)
Yellow is marked by relationships new
Taking on responsibility, deciding what to do.
A career and a family,
you work, play hard and struggle,
To make a living and move on,
many parts to juggle.

GREEN (34-44)
Then green comes along
and causes you to re-look,
To review the journey so far,
to assess the contents of your life's book.
You can now see what is missing

and what to put right,
to make up for lost time,
to take up the good fight.
You restate your goals and are ready to proceed,
Realizing you are getting older
and sense an urgent need.

BLUE (45-55)
Then before you know it, blue comes to reveal
The waning of the physical,
as the spiritual becomes more real.
You know you are here for some special reason
But need to discover it
before the end of the blue season.
The children are now gone, so you have more time
To start to find ways to commune with the divine.

INDIGO (56-66)
With indigo comes stature,
recognition and self worth,
knowing who you are
and why you came to planet Earth.
So you struggle to fulfill your mission
and do what needs to be done
to leave something good behind
in the dwindling years to come.

VIOLET (67-77 and beyond)
Till violet surprises you with its urgency at core
And keeps you trying to improve
and asking for more.
So then as the end approaches,
you know what life is about:
to discover your purpose and eradicate doubt,
to learn and assist others, to help lighten their load,
to grow quality and qualities on this earthly road.

An Essence Speaks

I

The Body

Here I am, oh human—
you have petitioned me to come and stay.
I trust your feelings are genuine
and won't be blown away.
I need you to give me fire food,
I need you to let me grow.
I need a constant safe home
and I need you to know.
Be a base and a companion,
through whom I can act and do;
If not you will have wasted my journey
and I will have to abandon you.

II

The Mind

So we have been together
and our union has managed to survive,
I see you have changed your ways of thinking
and you have kept me alive.
But don't assume, because you know me,
I'll be with you forever.
Restate often your agreement
so that we can continue to work together.

III

The Soul

Now we have merged into one
and cannot be parted;

we must work to complete
what we have started.
The journey is not finished
and we must do our best
to make every small moment count
as part of our quest.
Your life is connected but that does not say
that the future is certain, tomorrow or today.

My Religion

I am the best I have ever been;
grown up now—a childhood queen.
Dressed in purpose, a glowing crinoline;
The unseen magic of fairy tales
at last becomes seen.

The Kingdom of Wonder awaits me now;
A settlement to life that there is a quest—
a where, a what, and a how.
As the door opens and is left ajar,
I can sense the magic within, coming from afar.

The land of fairies I used to escape to before sleep
Becomes a knowing of what lives inside at deep.
The two merge into a discovery of what can be
If only I can let myself really be me.

August, 2002

Increase in Perception

I feel the wind with my hand
A gentle breeze blows through my fingers.
I feel the grass beneath my feet.
The warmth of the Earth radiates
through the soles of my feet
The Mother communion.

I feel the warmth of the sun upon my face.
I turn to meet it.
The gentle glow radiates towards the Earth.
It has taken eight minutes to get here.
The Father communion.

I raise my hands to feel the stars overhead.
I cannot do it with my hands,
I must do it with my mind.
I am still inside, I wait.
I feel a faint calling, a chorus of voices—
my brothers and sisters are calling me
and I am not alone.
A universal communion.

Qualities

Qualities
Introduction

The following poems are written with the idea that there are many levels of perception. When you think of a quality, there is the first understanding that comes to mind. And when you start thinking about it more deeply, you come to realize that there is much more to understand about it than you at first might have thought possible. Thus writing about a quality can be a never ending search and discovery that will lead a person from level to level and from understanding to understanding.

These poems are attempts at following such a search and trying to find new levels of perception that will then lead to further discovery and new questions. The results are never definitive, for there are many ways of looking at an object, a situation or a quality. There is no right or wrong in this, but these poems will hopefully promote and provoke the reader into finding his or her further perceptions and understandings.

Take, for example, a vase. It can be seen as a receptacle for flowers or it can be used to hold water or it can become a storage place for other objects, like pens or knitting needles. It all depends how you look at it. Of course, interpreting physical objects has its limitations and usually there are only a few uses we can put any object to at any one time. However, as far as qualities are concerned, there are many ways of looking at each one and no two people have the same experience of that quality, and therefore each person would probably come up with a different definition, if asked.

These writings are the author's attempts to find further definitions and new ways of looking at such qualities as peace, forgiveness, sublimation or generosity. It is like peeling off layers of an onion, always finding something new to think about and something new to understand.

This exercise is like climbing a ladder of perception and the interesting thing about it is that the higher you go, the greater the similarity between these qualities. It is almost as if there might come a point when all these qualities merge into an unseen plasma that allows a person to connect to higher states and to better understand the manifestation of the divine on earth.

Forgiveness

At first I regret the many wrongs I have done
Then I am sorry and wish they would go away—
each and every one.
Next there's an apology
and the attempt to reconcile.
So we make up and end it with a smile.
I then resolve— "this I will never ever repeat!"
I recognize my mistakes
and give myself a clean sheet.
I then have value for all that I have learned,
And see that mistakes made
are lessons honestly earned.
At the next level the quality mercy
dropeth like rain from above.
So I learn to say thank you (merci)
and deal with my weaknesses with love.
And finally atonement lives with me for real
As I learn about forgiveness
and how to start fresh and heal.

Leadership

At first a leader is a searcher, looking for a way;
Then he makes a decision
what to discard and what will stay;
Next he brings together
the threads that will last;
Then he holds the best of a person
from the future and the past;
Further he creates an ecology
within which others can win;
He then becomes a visionary
and makes many plates spin.
Then he guarantees what he will not go below;
At the next level he connects to high essences
that by contagion can grow;
Then he allows others
to make their own mistakes,
like a patient parent,
he knows what development takes.
Finally he responds to the universe
according to needs
and leads by example—he is a planter of seeds.

Trust

At first trust means I surrender to sleep
and believe that I will awake.
Then with deliberation I choose who to trust and why
and which path is best to take.
Consequently I begin to trust myself
to be true to my word and deed.
Which leads me to trust that I will be there
in a friend's greatest hour of need.
With increased vision I trust I can help the world
and see what I can best do.
With experience I trust my visions
and that they will one day come true.
Then will I trust the rules
by which my life can well progress.
This encourages me to trust that I should
do more of what I do best.
Then I trust the time has come
to review the status quo.
And finally I trust the Gods
to direct me where I next should go.

Generosity

At first it is a way of continuous giving;
Then it is a choice to pay back for living;
Next it is a natural response to need;
As it leads me to help others and abolishes greed;
Then it is an investment
that will come back one day;
Intuitively it connects to Creation
and sees there is a price to pay;
This causes an increase in generosity
for generosity's sake;
And then it demands a review
of the relationship between give and take;
At the next level it wants to be right in Creation's way;
Finally it is an embassy
and teaches me to pray.

Understanding

At first understanding wants to be understood;
Then it examines what it can
and what it should;
Next it looks out to see
a large world out there;
So it comes to feel others and learns to compare;
Then it puts itself in the picture
and looks for a plan;
Causing it to look in the mirror and see that it can;
Then it appreciates the unseen worlds
in its domain;
So that it may understand that
no two moments are the same;
Next it takes a higher view
to see what is right;
And finally it dedicates itself
to bring light into the night.

Sublimation

At first it means to try to improve;
And so it will challenge, question and move;
Then it connects distant and separate parts;
Next it inspires through healing and the arts;
Then it is an initiative that will see it through;
Intuitively it suggests there is so much more to do;
Then it becomes clear a life is a journey with an aim;
So it makes an attempt to align with the Universe
and become same-same;
With this there is the responsibility
for every thought and deed;
And finally life is a prayer
in response to Creation's needs.

Hospitality

At first I invite you to come round;
When you do, I listen to your words
and am sensitive to your sound;
So then I receive your radiation
in a same-same understanding way;
And try to say what I mean and mean what I say;
Next I fulfill your wish
and share with you what is mine;
So I can anticipate your need at a level that is fine;
This teaches me to have value for what lives
behind your eyes;
So that I am open and ready for a surprise;
Next I try to be colorless,
allowing you to be free to be you;
And finally I see a spirit in everything you do.

Art

At first art is everything and everything is art;
Then it educates
and there is a message it attempts to impart;
Next it distills the best
from any art form known;
To then add inspiration
and a quality that is all its own;
At this point it influences the world
to be a better place;
Then it reaches for the future
and creates a new mental space
for understanding and revelation
that then become norm;
At the next level it advances again
to create original content and form;
Finally it becomes timeless,
surviving through countless generations;
And is history in the making,
as it elevates and moves nations.

Peace

At first peace is the absence of stress
"I need some peace," we may say in distress.
Then again it appears
when you do what you do best—
It is you and it, oblivious to the rest.
Next you can find it in special secret places;
At the next level it lives in loved ones
and those dear, remembered faces.
"Rest in peace," you will say
as you bid them farewell
And gather in shared grief, with stories to tell.
Or "Peace be with you" at the time of goodbye
As you part and depart, with a tear and a sigh.
It then springs to action as it heals,
refreshes and renews;
Next it becomes creative
and inspires like a Muse.
When ready, it emerges into the world
to influence the written and spoken word;
To then incarnate into deep and powerful truths
that are rarely ever heard;
As it grows in power it brings an end to wars
and makes people come to their senses;
It will finally prevail
as we learn to trust it and lower our defenses.

Freedom

At first freedom is the ability to do;
Next it is to take something that exists
and make it brand new;
Then it gives rise to alliances vast;
Which will bring relationships together that will last;
Then it announces itself and stakes a claim;
To become a slavery to its chosen aim;
Gathering strength, it opens up horizons new;
To be able to connect to qualities
accessible to few;
It then acquires the power to protect
and serve the mission of its choice;
Finally it gives to receive
and knows the meaning of rejoice.

*My chosen name is Ora. Here are twelve reasons why I have chosen
this name:*

Ora

At first Ora is to do with time
In the sense that this is the moment to do;
Then it points to all that's sublime
To do with speech traveling from me to you;
The next level gives choice—between that and these
A choice that surrenders to known priorities.
In Hebrew it's light, Lord illumine me
So that I can make a true return to Thee.
An anagram says it is a tool—
an oar to row my boat ashore
A way to always search for more and more and more.
The word is a twinning of the sun and the Earth
And to a new me it will surely give birth.
At Easter Island it is a guardian of the mysterious past
And the quality of guardianship
I hope to help make last.
In Latin I see it is a prayer
Which opens up connections layer after layer.
Then it is an aim to pay tribute to Or
To immortality it opens up the door.
In Maori ora is a word that means health
Which helps me remember the price of real wealth.
The French say it's gold, which gives me a chance
To rewrite what is old,
To correct and enhance.
If you add a French key, you can make a new word—
It foretells the future in whispers rarely heard.

*The first level refers to the Polish word pora—
time, as in "it's time."
Second level—Ora as in oral, oratory and oration*

Third level—Or a (as in making a choice)
Fourth level—Or—light in Hebrew
Fifth level—Oar—anagram of Ora
Sixth level—O Ra—O representing the planet and Ra being the
Egyptian god of the sun
Seventh level—Ora—the name of the Easter Island statues
Eighth level—Ora—to pray in Latin
Ninth level—Or as in the name of the planet—Or or Ors
Tenth levl—Ora—health in Maori
Eleventh level—Or—gold in French—preserving the best of what
has been written in history
Twelfth level—add clé (key in French) and you get oracle.

Acceptance and Rejection

I accept I am frail and there's much I do not know
I accept I am weak and have a long way to go
I accept I am here with a mission to fulfill
I believe this process reveals the truth and is very real
I accept there are many, many paths to find
I accept it takes a lifetime to become ready and refined.

I reject the doubts that come up
when I can't see the way ahead
I reject criticism and ask for assessment instead
I reject the sense of loneliness
when friends are far away
For they are really close by each and every day.
I reject the feeling that I cannot carry on
With knowing that I am writing
my own unique live song.

I am learning a new skill—how to choose
and blend and sift
And to accept my life as a blessing and a gift.

The Vision

Dedicated to the North American Homestead, a spiritual community established in Tennessee in 2002.

I am a little person of God
Sometimes quite normal, and sometimes very odd.
I want to help put this planet right
To re-invoke the true essence of Lady and Knight.

I see a new world where the best will survive
Where honor and dignity again become alive
With a new meaning and stature, with development real
The ability to clair-see, clair-know and clair-feel.

Intuition becomes active and natural law dictates;
Compassion embodies true Samarital states.
Communication is energy of the human kind
And people gather together
to share what's on their mind.

Only actions progressive have a chance to succeed
And no one is hungry, no pressing desperate need.
To commune with the unseen which now gently appears
To help arrive at the next stage and overcome fears.

Healing is possible—the sun, sea and land
Being home to angels, touched by human hand.
All is charged beyond what anyone ever knew before
Even in ancient myth, religion and lore.

The Homestead is a heart with many unseen wires
Transferring conductivity and igniting new fires
Creating templates and outposts—
new centers, more space
Essences continue to gather in this religious place.

Qualities Meditation

Part One
When you are at you best, what qualities do you embody (name 3-7)?

Part Two
Choose one of the qualities.
Define it—what does it mean to you?

Part Three
Find words or expressions to decribe this quality at different levels.

Part Three
Re-define this quality, taking into account the many expressions defined in Part Three and not looking at the definition that you came to in Part Two.

Part Four
Find stories or experiences illustrating this quality.

Part Five
Compare your two definitions.
Share your results with others.

Creation Gives, the Human Responds

A One Act Play

Narrator:
Creation the giver, a ray of new birth
Is sent to evolve a new process on Earth.
The human responds within the permission
To take up, or not, the evolutary mission.

Creation:
This planet I create is a stage for giving
For the human to find a reason for living;
I see the need to create this home for two—
An ecology for both genders—the Green and the Blue.

The Planet:
My way is to support everything you do,
Not to judge or question, but be mother to you.
With persistence and care I give you a place
To be what you are, to create your electrical face.
I want nothing for myself, but for you to know
That this is a safe place in which you can grow.

The Boy:
Throughout my childhood I received so much,
Care, training and learning, the warmth of a touch,
Security and food, and an urge to know,
Allowance to discover, encouragement to grow.

The Girl:
Throughout my childhood I received so much,
Care, training and learning, the warmth of a touch,
Security and food, and an urge to know,
Allowance to discover, encouragement to grow.

The Man:
The gifts then continued when I was twenty
Given choices galore, a table of plenty.
Developing skills and learning to share
The man inside me wanted life to be fair.

The Woman:
The gifts then continued when I was twenty
Given choices galore, a table of plenty.
Developing skills and learning to share
The woman inside me wanted life to be fair.

The Man:
And then something else began to appear
An awareness that needed to be cured of its fear.
To touch originality, to give and receive
I just wanted desperately to be able to believe,
To know somewhere and somehow there is a way
To pass on the giftings and to be able to pay.

The Woman:
And then something else began to appear
An awareness that needed to be cured of its fear.
To touch originality, to give and receive
I just wanted desperately to be able to live,
To know somewhere and somehow there is a way
To return the giftings and to be able to pay.

The Man:
A lady I see is different to me
I look in her eyes and what do I see?
A universe looks out, a gift from afar
Perhaps from Creation or from a bright star.

The Woman:
A man I see is different to me
I look in his eyes and what do I see?
A universe looks out, a gift from afar
Perhaps from the sun or from a bright star.

The Man:
Physical possessions I really have none,
All is on loan, except what I have won
An essence is anchored, combined and mixed
Given expression, fluid, not fixed.
So I give to you all that I own
That on our sojourn on Earth we may not be alone.

The Woman:
I'm glad to receive, honored to serve—
Creation needs two, a dual God-nerve.
Thank you for sharing your most precious spark;
Together we dance and make a new mark.

Narrator:
Thus begins a new mental birth
A signal arises, transmitted from Earth;
Original and new, pristine and clean,
Creation sees itself as it has never been seen.

Creation:
Yes, I see emanating a very bright light
The Green and the Blue illuminate the night.
An original signal disperses the dark
And goes back to God as a coding, a spark.

The End

Earth Poems

Childhood
(The Planet Speaks)

Into the forest and over the bridge,
Climb up the hill and follow the ridge
There you will see the village below
And the winding river, moving so slow.

Pause for a minute and think of the time
When you were little and you were mine.
All was new and all a surprise
All was a feast for your open eyes.

Remember the thirst, how eager you were
To play and discover? It's all now a blur.
So try to connect to the search and the awe,
try to discover my planetary law.

The child is waiting, willing to play
Give it the time to extend its stay;
And you will hear the song of the Earth—
A second chance for a second birth.

The Planet's Lament
Earth Day

Thank you for the Earth Day
Thanks for being true,
Thanks for thinking green in May
And thanks for feeding "blue."*

Thanks a lot for planting trees
And those who care, I thank
Thanks for leaflets, books and treatise,
Sponsored by the Corporate Bank!

Thank you for your speech and tome,
By those who travelled far and near,
for I provide you with a home
Every day of every year.

So if you really want to help me—
Don't push me to the brink;
Find ways and means to understand me,
And change the way you think!

May 10, 1992

* *In Totonto, where this poem was written, 'blue' is the name of a blue plastic box for recycling.*

The Colors of Fall

As the leaves fall off the tree,
There is something new to see.
Blue and yellow make the green
But when it is no longer seen,
blue retracts leaving yellow on its own;
The leaves are now dry to the bone
The blue water has gone and the leaves fall—
Considering the colors, it is no mystery at all.

Without the blue, the red will appear
Bringing the power of fire near.
Throughout the summer, blue held it back
Now it takes over for a short spark.
Then when the fire of autumn dies down,
the leaves are burnt to the color brown.
The final leaf falls to the ground.
Thus on its way down, brown meets brown.
And with the final dimming of the light
All colors of autumn are coated with white.

Mother of Renewal

Oh Mother of Renewal,
be my teacher, be my guide
Show me how I can forgive
and how to harness pride.
You somehow bear the ills and wrongs,
misguided deeds of men and men...
If I were you, there would be no now
or today or tonight or then and then...
If you were me, I'd find a way
and start again and yet again...
If we were one, with every spring
our breath and birth would be our creed
If I had a fraction of your compassion,
I could respond to those in need.
Oh Mother, teach me, show me,
lead me, be my guide
And I will surely learn to harness pride.
Oh Mistress of Renewal,
show me how you can
Forgive the pain and carry on
With your greater plan.

January 1, 1999

The Summer Flower

Ah, here it comes—
my finest day and my finest hour.
I last but for a short time,
for I am a summer flower.
I wait all year for my brief moment
of my next appearance—
And then I am the ballerina,
as on my chosen spot I dance.

Every year I wait, prepare,
until the time is right;
And then I push against the earth,
to birth into the light.
Oh glory, happiness, reward—
that moment so divine
When the whole wide world can see me—
the prize is truly mine.

So even though it's short, it's sweet
and makes me work all year
And all my instinct is alerted
when the time draws near.
Nature dresses me in hues
of red and green and blue;
My moment lasts but for a season,
and then I say adieu.

But you—with two legs and a brain,
your time lasts for so long;
And you can walk and run and jump,
you can think and sing your song...
Remember me when times are tough
and in your darkest hour;
Remember how much more you do
than the summer flower.

The River

River, oh river, where have you been?
River, oh river, what have you seen?
River, oh river, what is your aim?
And will you always remain the same?

Oh human, you ask and I shall reply
I have but one aim under the sky
To get to where my future is due
To join to the ocean, the great waters blue.

I have been flowing for many a-year
And always the purpose and journey is clear
I know where I'm going, I know what to do;
In that I'm so much more fortunate than you.

Oh river, my friend, I will ask you again
I know where you're going,
I know how, what and when.
But when you do get there,
you'll no longer be you,
Lost in the ocean, the great waters blue.

Oh human, oh bright one, surprisingly slow
There's one thing I trust and one thing I know
When I join something greater, I benefit too
For my destiny becomes one
with the great waters blue.

So before I move on, I have one thing to say—
Live for tomorrow, but do it today.
And don't hesitate to join things greater than you
And you can become the Great Waters Blue.

Written on the bank of the Nottawasaga River, Ontario
January 2, 1998

I Must Be Like the Water

I
I must be like the water
And find my own level
To then forge my way
to the sea of knowledge and experience
And to carry nourishment
and refreshment to those in need.

II
I must be like the air
Invisible to what needs to move through me,
Light and accessible to all parts of me
With a cool breeze blowing.

III
I must be like the earth
Supportive and constant
to that which I uphold
and what upholds me.
Growing the seeds of my development
Offering stability to the ever changing,
dancing, moving
expressions of the day.

IV
I must be like the fire
burning bright
with intention and belief,
illuminating a path as I go
and learning the art of self cleansing.

V
And then there is the time
when these four become three.
In a special place, a special moment
the mergings happen
when I am no longer like
the water, the air, the earth, the fire;
I am the water, the air, the earth, the fire,
and they are me
and together we are
the servants and expressions
of what is possible.

Thank You

Thank you for the water
Thank you for the air
Thank you for the earth
And thank you for the care.

I see beauty everywhere:
The beauty of the autumn trees,
The beauty of a flock of geese,
The beauty of a blade of grass,
The beauty of the days that pass.

All were touched by the Creator's hand—
The sky, the air, the sea, the land.
All were colored with the Creator's touch
Showing that she cares so much.

Now here is something I cannot deny:
If they are beautiful, then so am I.

Writings from the Desert

These writings were produced during a five-day trip to the Negev Desert in Israel, meditating and sharing concepts and understandings associated with the idea of human warmth.

The trip was organized by Desert Journeys, located in the village of Ma'ale Zvia in the Galilee, Israel.

Com-Passion—
the many ways of giving

A tree grows—it is given permission
It gives shade
It gives nutriments
It gives the seeds of its continuance
It provides levels for the little people of the planet
to find their place
It connects to and transmits energy from other planets,
thus enhancing the Earth's array of available influences
It teaches the lesson of continuance, variety
and faithfulness
It is a symbol of steadfastness and durability
It is a custodian of history
It is home for many creatures, large and small
Even when it perishes, it provides warmth and shelter
It gives raw material for human shelter,
convenience and beauty
It is a feeding funnel for the planet
It connects the elements of air to the elements of earth
and vice versa
It cleans the air and the atmosphere of the planet
It is the planet's lungs
It heals and gives raw material
for healing and medicinal purposes
It provides clues as to the ecology and its surroundings

*It is a transmitting station for planetary and human
generated essences
It communicates with others of its kind, thus being
a living example of telepathy and clairvoyance
It also provides the service of transmitting
communications for and from the little people
and the big people of the planet
It is the source of numerous herbal remedies,
known from ancient times and as yet unknown
It contains the wisdom of the ancients.*

How many ways of giving do I practice?

A Call-over
Asking for warmth

*Give me the warmth that melts the ice of separation
from all that is refined and that supports human,
planetary and universal evolution.*

Many Warmths

There are many kinds of warmth, so really there should be many words to describe them. Each warmth allows a connection, a bonding, a binding, a joining. Different to the kind of warmth measured by the increase in temperature, the following types of warmth allow for the exchange of energy and endearment.

Human Warmth
Humans come together to share their contents and their passions within the presence of warmth.

Angelic Warmth
Warmth is needed to connect to an entity or angel, for like humans, they will respond to the warmth that inspires a response.

Planetary Warmth
Then there is planetary warmth, which a human can connect to when he or she considers the planet and her needs. When a sympathetic note is reached, the planet may respond, offering in return enhancement and encouragement.

Universal Warmth
Then there is universal warmth, which is invitational to entities above planetary level. It is the stuff our spirit is made of and when generated by the human, these two—the human and the universe—can merge and down this line revelation, connection and power can travel one way and service, gratitude, consideration and support up the other.

Give

The mother gives continuously. It is how she grows.
To give is to receive.
The whole universal system is designed towards
GROWTH, though individual parts may die, when they
are no longer fit to serve the whole, to then be transformed
into usefulness.

The path towards growth is therefore clear:

Give to receive
Give to promulgate the essence of generosity
in the world
Give to contribute to growth, for if the planet grows,
you grow, too
Give to learn from the experience of giving
Give to confirm the universal urge to grow
Give to connect to the universe and to do as it does
Give to confirm the planet
Give to honor your life and that which created you
Give to be in service to God.

Farewell to the Desert

With warmth we have danced for five days now
Many small steps to attempt to learn how—
An exercise, a sharing, a tasking, a chat—
Learning from each other, trying this and that.

We have discovered the desert is our brother
We have found richness in listening to each other
Many new friends and people of kind
New revelations to open the mind.

Today the time has come to return home
Knowing with certainty we are never alone
Taking impressions, memories and the will to be
With the domain of warmth as a reality.

Child's Play

The following poem was written as a result of a meditation about the planet we live on and our own involvement in the greater universal plan.

Musings About Life, the World and Me

Introduction

My thoughts are as fishing rods,
drawing what I want near
The more I contemplate the universe, the more it is I hear.
Its music plays a divine and haunting sound...
I hear it when alone, with no one else around.

Connection comes with patience, persistence, prayer
The depth of connection reveals layer after layer
The more I listen,
the more there is to know and do and think;
It summons me to work,
to write my future in endelible ink.

What Is the Weight of the Pacific Ocean?

I
I need to know the answer now
I need to get to it somehow
How much does the Pacific Ocean weigh?
Give or take a couple of pounds. What do you say?

See a globe inside your mind
To view the ocean and to find
How long, how wide, how deep, how blue...
This is what you have to do.

Then do the math and add the sums,
How many gallons, how many tons?
In your mental ship take flight
And search the answer that is right.
It does not matter if you take all day,
It does not matter what you say.
Just try to add up all that weight
And it will bring you to the gate.

To the brink where value lives
Where revelation yields and gives,
Appreciation waits to come
And join the process when it's done.

So struggle, work it, up the pace
Think of water, air and space,
So enormous is this Earth,
To all you see it's given birth.

If you were Atlas, strong and tall,
Could you lift it—earth and all?
Could you hold it in your hand?
And upon what surface would you stand?

So in your mind take a great big cup
And with the ocean, fill it up.
How big would that mug need to be?
And how many bags to make some tea?

All these questions taunt my brain
As I try to answer, solve, explain...
Each new riddle opens up the door,
To thoughts and curios, more and more.

II

I am made of earthly matter
And when I die all that will scatter,
To build another living form
To start again—that is the norm.
I am mostly H2O
How much exactly, I do not know.
How many me's to fill a sea?
What is the difference between it and me?

If I were a part of the ocean blue,
Would it make a difference to what I do?
My weight is small, my size not large
But like the ocean, I can hold a charge.

The world is huge and yet so small
That in my mind I see it all.
We are partners on this trip
As I sail the ocean on a ship.

I can swim and drink and move along,
I can watch the waves and hear their song,
I can feel the strength and love the power
Of a drop of rain or a summer shower.

Water, water, we are one,
Bound together till our work is done.
Cleaning, cooling, adding hue...
We are united in the cosmic stew.

So I am small and you are great—
So different when you measure weight.
But when you think of our endeavor,
We are universal expressions, both together.

III

Around the world go and see
So many things—a rock, a tree...
I pick up a stone and test its weight
A bucket of water... I pause, I wait.
If I could add the weight of trees,
Could I work it out with ease?
Mountains, rivers, fields and dales,
They all weigh something, but who has the scales?

Who can weigh the worldly mass
And add the unseen, air and gas,
All the elements, old and new—
I don't know who; perhaps it's you!

IV

Responding to a god's demand
A giant once held the world in his hand
"I think this one is rather small,"
He said, for he was very tall.

"I could throw it into space
Or take it to another place
Another galaxy, another sky.
Tell me what you want and why.

"Where do you want it, where should it go?
Should it rotate fast or slow?
How long should it rotate around the sun?
And how long should it stay there, once it's begun?"

"Third from the sun," the answer came,
"Maybe it's small, but all the same
It has an important part to play
As it travels along its eminent way."

V

One tiny speck, a dot, a mark,
Here for a moment, an interim spark...
The world goes on for millions of years...
The human is born, lives and disappears.
A few little drops, a bit of weight
Is all we are in our physical state.
Alone and small, light and brief
But large in potential, strong in belief.

Inside a seed awaiting the light
A spark, though small can burn very bright
The spirit is weightless, but it has the power
To ignite the system in its flaring hour.

It can grow and contage, inspire and teach;
It can connect to the stars, extend outwards and reach
The highest of high, the deepest of deep.
It can hold onto a secret, protect in its keep.

But when you have the code and can open its lock,
With value and depth, you will remove the block.
You can enter its realms and know what it knows;
You can learn about life and how the universe grows.

You will feel value and mystery in all that you meet,
Never guilty or afraid, no need to retreat.
There is learning to gain from a leaf or a stone
There is comfort and sharing
when you're no longer alone.

Lighter Fare

The Bread Maker

The dough is churning, churning, churning
On its journey, journey, journey
Towards a bread.

From the beginning, beginning, beginning
We are spinning, spinning, spinning
Until we are dead.

The planet's turning, turning, turning
On her journey, journey, journey
Around the sun.

We are learning, learning, learning
On this journey, journey, journey
Until we are one.

Around, around, around we go
Whirling, taking, baking, learning,
For how long I do not know;
Churning, waking, making, yearning
On this never ending journey.
Wholewheat, sourdough, corn or rye
You won't know until you try.
So come along and join the fun
See what you are when you're done:
Crumpet, bagel, pretzel, bun?

April 10, 1998

Two Clocks

A clock that is going might be slightly wrong,
A few minutes past the hour it will chime its song.
As much as it tries, it can't quite catch up
To tell its owner when to wake
or when it's time to sup.
Or perhaps it tends to speed ahead,
it's going much too fast
To give the answer when to bed
Or how long to break the fast.
But a clock that has ceased to work
will be right twice a day.
"I know time better than you,"
it will gloatingly say.

A Voice

Anne Louise lost her luggage
and she wondered why,
What could God have against her
in his home in the sky?
She always tried so hard
and did so many things well,
And yet her red case was not coming out again
onto the dreaded carousel.
What have I done wrong? Why is it always me?
Others have picked up and gone
with two bags or even three.
Oh, why is life so cruel, when to others it is kind?
And then she heard a little voice whisper,
"You must learn not to mind!"

A Good Deed

There is a thing I do
that to some may seem coarse
It has nothing to do with groundwork,
or healing or the force.
Yet the God life in me has a chance to rejoice
When I walk into a public washroom
and make a decisive choice.

It goes like this:
Here is your chance
to make things better than before
Just pick up the toilet paper
that is littering the floor,
Wipe down the sink
so others can have a clean start,
And put waste paper in the garbage.
There, you have played your part.

The Pool—A Lament

By A. Blade

My home has been excavated,
I have nowhere to go
Nowhere for a poor blade of grass to grow
A hole in the earth where there used to be plants,
Covered in concrete; no worms and no ants.
I gave up my life for her and for him,
So in their spare time they can go for a swim.

A Problem

I have a little bit of a problem
I have forgotten where "you" ends and "I" begin.
I have also forgotten where "I" end
and "you" begin.
So when I say "you" I no longer know
who I am addressing—me or you?
And when you say "I,"
are you talking about me or you?

And when I look at you, am I looking at me?
When I think I know better, do I really?
When I speak to the many parts of me,
do they serve me or you or both?
For a kidney is a kidney,
a brain is a brain
and a heart is a heart.
Can I really claim possession of my organs?
If I saw my heart, would I know it was mine?
Or would I think it was yours?

Perhaps I can substitute the word "human"
for me and you and then the problem will end.
Or a new one will begin, because
I would no longer know where we end
and everything else begins.

Gender Writings

Women Carrying Water

Women carrying water—
through the jungle and the plains
Women nurturing others and bearing childbirth pains
Women connecting to the Earth
and feeling her silent cry
Women upholding dedication
so great qualities will never die.

Women carrying water—it nourishes and revives
Women offering healing to unguided and lost lives
Women carrying water—
but behold, it's changed its state
It's wine that carries a charge, before it is too late.

Hope

I believe that we ladies are tasked to be custodians of hope to hold and protect it for the benefit of all humankind — both men and women — until there is a respect and safety into which we will be able to release it like a dove from a cage into the world.

Hope that is not based in wishful thinking or unreasonable demands, but comes from and is nurtured by a deep and powerful connection to the universal intelligence that has a vision and a plan as far as the evolution of the human race is concerned.

Hope that is not personally based, but is powered by a long line of human endeavor, stretching into the millions of years and passed down to us in our time within the astral light of the planet, within electrical signals accompanying great works of art, architecture, music, literature, science and so many expressions of the indomitable human spirit.

Hope that looks to the future with certainty and optimism and belief that humanity and peace will prevail.

This hope is a plasma of readiness, eager to embrace the future, offering it a fitting anchor and welcoming foundation.

Hope

Thus will I be a temple where hope can reside
A fitting sanctuary, still and intact inside
It's not that I hope, but that hope lives with me
So that one day we both can set it free.

August 28, 2006

For the Gentlemen

Salute the Gentleman

I am grateful that the gentleman life still exists on planet Earth and that there are those who have upheld the possibility of this level of development, mostly abandoned and not promulgated into the future. How can a woman be a lady without a man, any man, attempting to be a gentleman?

And conversely, how can a man be a gentleman without a woman, any woman, attempting to be a lady?

Occult connections at the level of lady/gentleman await and there is such an honor and courage in the commitment to this path. I salute your intention and rejoice on behalf of all females who are now being born into a world where there are those who uphold and wish to protect the living manifestation of both genders.

Westchester, January 18, 2004

The following writing was a keynote speech delivered at the "Humanity and Gender" conference organized by Feminenza in partnership with UNESCO PEER and held at the UN compound in Nairobi, Kenya in January, 2005.

Redefining Femininity

The idea of femininity has been an evolving concept through the ages. Also, each person, each culture and tradition has their own idea of how this translates into a form, a picture or an idea.

Here's the Oxford definition of feminitity:
1) Feminine quality; the characteristic quality or assemblage of qualities pertaining to the female sex, womanliness; in early use also, female nature.
2) In depreciative sense: womanishness
3) In applied senses:
    a. the fact of being a female.
    b. feminine peculiarity (in shape)
4) Women in general: womankind

This doesn't seem to be very helpful.
So I asked different men to tell what they saw femininity to be and I received many different answers, mostly appealing to four of the five senses—sight, sound, touch and smell—with words such as:
Soft
Nicely turned out
Things in their proper place
A good smell
Soft spoken.

Then there was a feeling beyond the five senses that translates as alluring, attractive.

If we could go back in history and ask the same question, we would receive a whole array of different answers. Throughout history the evolving idea of femininity has been expressed by great artists, known and unknown, as they paid tribute through their art to their idea of beauty and femininity. Even different parts of the body were accentuated at different times.

In different parts of the world this evolving story has been portrayed in various ways. The idea of femininity has found its expression in the different dances that evolved in different parts of the world. So from belly dancing in the Middle East to the hula in the Pacific islands, to Irish dancing or the defiant spirit of the Flamenco, which had its origin in Spain when it was overrun by Moors, to Thai dancing and tribal African dances—each expresses a different idea of femininity and accentuates different parts of the body, enhanced by costume, head dresses, color and gesture.

I believe we are in a time of femininity evolution and it is this generation's tasking to redefine the word. Definitions in a dictionary are dead—fossilized witnesses to past ideas and processes. However, language is alive and the words are still evolving and as we live, we are rewriting language and redefining the ideas and thoughts that are attached to each word and phrase. It feels to me like this is a time to scoop up the ideas of past ages, which are so accessible today thanks to the technology of the Internet, computer, movies, radio, TV—and to extract the best, bringing it together into a new idea of femininity.

So, looking at history of art and into the future, three levels of femininity can be distinguished:

1. *Femininity based on the beauty and appeal of the female form; the worship of the ability of the woman to have children. This idea of femininity has been physical in its nature and glorified the prevailing ideal from ancient times until the onset of the Renaissance. It can be seen in ancient anonymous carvings, in Greek statues and Medieval pictures. Beautiful, silent women, obedient, child bearing, bountiful.*

2. *Femininity as expressed by the awakening female character—intelligent, independent and strong minded. This image began to appear during the Renaissance in Europe and developed during the Industrial Revolution, when women came out of the homes to work in factories and offices. This evolving image reached its peak during the two World Wars when women constituted the majority of the work force, occupying positions at all levels of management, proving their capability and resourcefulness. So this type of femininity is based in skills, abilities, talents and action—women doing what they love to do and what they are good at, unhindered and free. The evolution of this femininity, which I shall call Femininity Two, led inevitably to women obtaining the vote and occupying in some countries the highest office in the land.*

3. *Today we are in the midst of a further evolution. This is the dawning of Femininity Three. Not based in the physical or in their skills, it encompasses Femininity One and Two and adds another layer to this emerging picture. Femininity needs to take another step up the evolutionary ladder to prepare for the future and to be responsive to the needs of tomorrow. Its hallmark consists of rare qualities, such as humanity, compassion, forgiveness, generosity etc. with the ability to lead, teach*

and translate the new signals that are influencing this planet from the universe, creating a need to find new expressions in everything we believe, think and do.

The new woman needs to be brave but not arrogant, persistent but not aggressive, understanding but not compromising, willing but not weak. There is a huge tasking awaiting us and this is just the beginning. It requires dedication and belief from both genders, because the idea of femininity cannot evolve without the evolution of the idea of masculinity. And like a puzzle, both need to fit together to become a foundation on which the future can anchor.

The following writing was part of a ceremony, held on my 62nd birthday and witnessed by family and friends.

The 9 Gifts and the 10 Blessings

I believe that all life is purposeful, including mine. I believe that we have been given all the gifts necessary to proceed, to learn, to understand why we are here:

The gift of consciousness
The gift of reason
The gift of intelligence
The gift of detection
The gift of comparison
The gift of acceptance
The gift of denial
The gift of choice
The gift of continuance.

As time moves on, and more and more of my life is written, the years and months and days become urgent and important and magnified. It is like being under a crystal dome wherein I am surrounded by beauty and love. I see beauty everywhere and I am grateful for the many gifts bestowed upon me.

The blessing of loved ones
The blessing of friends
The blessing of nature
The blessing of thought
The blessing of inspiration
The blessing of revelation
The blessing of art and music and dance
The blessing of sharing
The blessing of giving
The blessing of a value added life.

Being a Woman
(A Monologue)

I am a woman. Yes, that's obvious and when you look at someone, what is the first thing you determine? Age, gender and appearance. So by now you have been able to assess that I am an older woman. It probably is also important to decide that I pose no threat—no need for a fight or flight reaction. So you are looking at me and you are probably wondering what this is all about.

Well, I am here to tell you that locked up in me are over 60 years' worth of experience, just as locked up in you are your years of experience as well. And within those years there have been many lives, many small lives and some large lives, too.

I think we make a mistake when we look at someone and say to ourselves—"Ah, there's a man; he's middle-aged, he's fat, or thin and he looks like a decent sort of chap." Then you get introduced and so now you have a label to attach to that image—say, Harry. So Harry gets defined, categorized and filed away somewhere in the catacombs of your brain.

Well, how would you like it if someone went to the file in their brain with your name on it, pulled it out and saw a little slip of paper with your gender, approximate age and perhaps your occupation, your marital status or a single assessment, like nice or flashy or boring... because that is what probably most people who have met you have filed away about you. Except the precious few who know you better and on whom you have made a greater impact, for better or for worse.

So gender. It is something that we are born with. It is determined at the moment of conception as soon as the sperm from your father impregnates your mother's ovum, somewhere in the darkness of one of your mother's fallopian tubes. It is the sperm that determines gender, as it carries either an X or a Y chromosome. As the female does not have a Y chromosome, it is only the male sperm that can carry either, and therefore its content decides whether it's going to be blue for a boy or pink for a girl.

So you end up belonging to one of the two kinds of humans on Earth—male or female, and already, as soon as you are born, there are differences. Not only are you expected to play with dolls, if you are a girl, and not dirty your clothes as much as the boys, but you are treated differently and expected to become a "young lady" and to behave "properly," or as befits a girl. Well, let's rewrite that from the start. A female child has two legs and two arms and at least some of them can climb trees quite well.

So female. That's my gender, that's what I am, at least for this lifetime. That is the foundation I have been given, very much like a canvas upon which to paint my unique portrait. During my first years I wasn't aware of the difference. When a small three-year-old boy and girl are playing naked on the beach, and one says to the other, "Guess what I am! A boy or a girl?" the other one replies, "I don't know. Get dressed and I'll tell you."

But then came puberty and I became very aware of my female body and how it was changing. It was a big event to start having periods and to feel my breasts growing. And to compare them to other breasts beginning to protrude from the chests of girlfriends at school. And then noticing after gym classes in the changing room how some girls were starting to wear bras.

The female body—that's how I can identify with the female part of me—the joys and pains of getting ready to receive. For it was not only my womb that was getting ready to receive, but I was getting ready at many levels—from physical, to emotional, to energy to spiritual. And then looking at boys in a completely different light. No longer playground companions, they seemed to be more interested in other aspects of our prospective interchange. Sure, we had seen most of what there was to see in the movies, we thought we knew what to expect, but what substitute is there for the real thing?

A whole new world opened up when I discovered boys. A new awareness was called into life and how sweet and bitter and exciting and stimulating it was. The blood in my veins was circulating faster and the mirror in our bathroom was being worn out by the hours I spent looking into it, experimenting with make up and thousands of hair-dos.

Alongside the body changes, there was another life waking up inside me—and she was 100% woman. More subtle than the female girl, not subject to dramatic mood swings, she had the foresight and intelligence to know what she wanted. Those were the years when for the first time I could begin to see what I wanted my life to become.

So at puberty was the first time when I began to sense and identify with more than one life inside me. I was a female with female needs and urges—wanting to be pretty and popular and integrated into a circle of friends. I was also becoming a woman with a mind of her own, her unique capabilities, and the ability to nurture and share. And then there was a third life, far more subtle and far seeing—the one that longed to improve and discover the spiritual dimension of living—beyond the physical needs of today or the ambitions of tomorrow. This was the delicate appearing life of feminine wisdom — the timeless one to whom time is a limitless yardstick of who she may become.

And throughout all stages of life there was and still is yet another life that belongs to the universe and is but a visitor here — the spirit that is hosted by the girl child, the woman and the crone (to mention three classical archetypes) — absorbing the results of the experiences fostered by the other three. She is the one that is connected to the universal house of the feminine gender that sends its tentacles and conduits throughout time and space to grace and enhance the livable expanse, supporting, complementing and supplementing the other gender, the masculine side of God, wherever and however it might appear.

One always breaks down into two and how privileged are we to represent by our very gender this highest of all universal laws, the law of duality. Inescapable as day and night, dawn and dusk, hot and cold, for as long as we live in a human body, we are fused and integrated into the divinity of the Law of Opposites, never again to feel alienated or distanced from the most sacred core of creational law.

But back to this planetary dance of the many lives within. As time moved on, more and more the wisdom of the woman took over, taking on responsibility for the well being and survival of the other lives within, as well as other lives outside of her that came to depend on her. She thus became the nurtuting mother and the provider, the giver of gifts, a role that is second nature to her.

Within the years of too much to do, this maternal woman became a manager and she developed hundreds of skills. She learned how to balance and combine so many tasks — earning a living, looking after a family, finding her way in the world—and all this while she was still growing up, and while she still needed attention and confirmation herself, and the higher part needed time to know for sure how she was going to protect herself on the one hand and share herself on the other.

Still vulnerable, but with a powerful potential, this universal team was getting ready to play its own unique tune of life.

All these lives arrived at the mid-point together—still struggling to establish harmony between them, but resilient and convinced that they were on a mission and that life was purposeful and that it required for them to take up its motto and banner, whatever that turned out to be. So that was the new tasking that opened up at this time of the mid-life opportunity. For the first time the road ahead cleared and looking back at the first half of life, it became obvious that in continuing along the same path in the same way, the scenery would not change, but would become a down-hill deterioration into old age and ultimately oblivion. Thus something else was needed to bring all these lives onto an elevated path, where development and refinement would become their companions and where a new spiritual energy awaited, motivating them to adopt a long view of life, stretching into the universe and eternity. So, rather than clinging to physical life, which the short-sighted love of youth and physical beauty—the temptation of the female girl—was persuading them to adopt, intuition and a longing for a spiritual life prevailed. This new quest brought with it a sense of enhancement and permanence that only rare quality can promote, and which the experience and wisdom of the years makes it possible to identify and consequently adopt into the whole.

So from then on life took on a whole new dimension whereby there was always an underlying longing for and appreciation of the intangible, the ineffable, which, although hard to describe, is more real than any human constructed edifice. And so as the menopause years drew near, it was a time of release from the planetary duty of giving birth, in preparation for the next life to come.

Viewed as the next stage on this journey, it was no longer a sign of the end of womanhood, but on the contrary—the beginning of the spiritual unification of all stages of life, traveling together into the certain, unknown, mysterious future where all that she will ever need or desire is here inside of her, waiting to be prized out and shared with those who have the sensitivity and need to find out what awaits them further up this road called life.

And so now in my 60s I delight at the intricacies of this universal dance as I move towards the last stages of my earthly journey. I can see clearly now where I have been and I am not alone, but always assisted and companioned by different aspects of my femininity, each of which brings with her her unique gifts and abilities. As long as the instructions are clear and the greater mission is in view, their varied needs will never clash for long, for all have taken a stance and made a commitment to be the best that they can be and to work tirelessly to rewrite feminine history as it appears in the world, adding to its now and its future the qualities that will allow the bloom of partnership between male and female, man and woman, the masculine and the feminine.

Cameo Writings

On Waiting

We think we know about waiting because we wait for a bus or we wait in the doctor's waiting room, and waiting seems to be a part of life in that we have heard such sayings as, "Wait for me" or "Wait until I give you something." And what does that conjure up in our minds? Because waiting is first of all to do with the anticipation of an event or occurrence that is expected to happen in the future.

However, where waiting gets dangerous is when it is associated with the idea of suspension or idleness. In other words, holding back one's activities or thought processes or the flow of one's life in anticipation of something that actually might never happen. For how many times have you waited for something that didn't take place, like, for example, standing on a street corner waiting for somebody who never came? Or waiting for an event that doesn't happen, or waiting for a job that doesn't materialize? So, if you draw a line and now is at one point on the line and the anticipated event is at another point on that line:

Now ————————————————— *anticipated event*

then the space between those two points could be called the waiting period. So the question here arises, what happens in our minds from the moment of anticipation to the moment of fulfillment, if such a moment indeed happens? Do we alter our state because we are waiting? This is where the idea of waiting successfully comes in, because if we suspend our normal going on, our activities, our ways of thinking, because something might happen in the future, then we are robbing ourselves of precious time, which could be put to productive use. Not only have we suspended the flow of our life, but after the anticipated event does or does not occur, it will take us time to re-engage in that flow and join the current of life.

Therefore, when we sit in a waiting room, waiting for the doctor, our life is still ticking by and that time is just as valuable as when we might be engaged in a favorite pursuit. So there must be ways whereby we can use that time to our own advantage, to our own progression, towards our own development, so that less gets wasted. Life is very short and, in a way, we are all waiting for that final event—death, because death can be anticipated with certainty.

So if we draw a line and on one point of the line is now and another point on the line is our own death:

Now ■━━━━━━━━━━━━━━━━━━━━━━━ death

then the period between the two is waiting for death. After all, death is the only event that we can absolutely guarantee, concerning our future. However, even knowing the fact that it is something we can be certain of does not necessarily cause us to stop and suspend our ambitions and activities, cancel our aims and desires, because we know they will inevitably come to an end, together with our time on Earth. Perhaps on the contrary, because we know that final moment is coming, we might feel an urgency to fit in as much as possible between now and then.

So, why would that be different from, for example, waiting for somebody or holding back until a person you are waiting for comes to join an activity or a meeting?

Surely the same principle can apply, in that time is always precious and we cannot have our time again.

Permission

Within the small band of human experience already appeared and within the very large band of human experience not yet appeared but potentially possible, experience is limited and defined on both sides—on one side by what the planet will allow (if a person jumps off a high building, they will perish), and, on the other side, by what the human will allow (if you murder someone and get caught in peace time, you will be imprisoned and your freedom will be taken away from you). Of course, for humans the law will vary from country to country within the greater laws of the planet which are uniform around the globe.

Within this band of two permissions (planetary and human) there are two divisions:

1. The first is what has already been filled out by human evolution and by human activity. So this covers everything that the human as a race and a specie has done. So, for example, all the sports records of the human race are recorded here. All the artistic achievements, the arts of expression, the ability to perform, to do, to work, to write, to speak—every single action or idea adds to this particular band.

2. Then there is a much wider part, which represents everything that the human has not yet done, but can do and perhaps will do with the help and ability of its present model. So this is where human evolution has brought us to and clearly is a shifting and changing picture, as each day passes and more experience becomes filled out by the human as a specie and a collective intelligence.

We are standing in between these two stages, pioneering that which has not yet been done (2), causing its diminishment, into the domain of that which has been done (1), instigating its increase. So, for example, in band 2 are all the inventions that have not yet been invented, perfecting what has already been done and what already exists (from inventing a new model of a television set to improving family life or inter-personal relationships), and pushing the limits of human physical achievements back to set new records. Thus next year's records lie in this band, and the year's after that and the year's after that. The boundaries of the human's current permission cause it to act within that seemingly narrow band that we are currently straddling. However, how large or narrow it really is, who can tell? Even at a personal level, how much better can you become at something you are already good at? How much more is there to learn, to discover, to accomplish, to know? And even as we learn, how much new knowledge appears every day, to be added to the libraries and college curricula of the world? The permission increases all the time, revealing the new.

Thus the picture of a band of permission within which the human finds itself is false to begin with, because we live (and always have lived) in moving, shifting and changing times. The permission increases as we fill out more of what is already possible and push back the limitations of that which has been given to us. For example, having acquired a new skill, we quickly learn of new depths and understandings connected with that skill or field of knowledge. Take for example, photography. A person can easily learn how to hold a camera and then go around the planet, looking for attractive places or faces to take pretty pictures. They will focus their eye (or the eye of the camera) on a scene and decide that it looks good and click, they will take a picture. However, perhaps after a while they will move from a planetary view to a sun level view and they will understand that the quality of light in their picture will give it depth, color and a new interest. This will open up a whole new experience and understanding of photography and they will go around looking for new ways in which the light illuminates and is reflected by objects and scenes, and in which objects reflect the light. This will be a much more subtle understanding of photography, for now they will be chasing the unseen and their pictures will reflect atmospheres and feelings, rather than physical objects only...

It is clear that every human being is born within the current band of permission, defined by natural law on the one hand and human law on the other and has the ability of fulfilling any number of possibilities therein. The human cannot transgress the band of planetary permission, even if it does not know exactly where its limits lie (for who knows what the ultimate record for running a mile really is?) and it will never, within one lifetime, fulfill all possibilities. This can only be done by the entire human race as a specie, over a long time. The human will continue to make its choices in its search for purpose and for the meaning of life.

If you write the word PERMISSION, thus: PER-MISSION, it becomes clear that within the limited permission of human life it is for each person and each individual to set their own mission and find their way to connect to the ionic charge that waits for those who push back the unknown, winning greater territory into the known. These are the real pioneers of our time.

When humans live their life with a purpose and choose a particular path amongst many, and make decisions as to how they are going to define their mission in life, it is at that moment that they will eliminate certain other paths and ways and means and actions that are open to them within the overall band of permission that will simply fall away untroden, unfulfilled and not taken up, as the person takes on direction in their life. So, for example, someone who decides to become a Catholic priest will possibly deny themselves the experience of marriage and parenthood. Or someone who has decided to become a doctor will have to dedicate a certain amount of time to their studies and practice and will therefore have less time for other things. So, the moment one takes on a mission, one will MISS IONS, one will not put energy into other things that do not come into the domain of that mission. One could think that this is a limitation of one's freedom, for one is further narrowing the band of permission within the already established band of human possibility. However, it could be looked at another way in that by choosing a particular path, one is opening up one's options within that narrower band and one is more able to exercise oneself within the domain of human permission, when looking at it from the standpoint of being a specie and having already achieved a certain amount of success or establishment. So therefore, someone who has decided to become, say, a physician, can then specialize within that possibility and choose to, for example, look into the domain of viruses and within that territory become not only a specialist, but also an inventor or a discoverer of a cure to a previously untreatable disease. Or they might travel to exotic places and become someone who rescues others from a debilitating illness. Thus, within the narrow band of their chosen MISSION, they will push back the barriers of human limitation and experience to fill out the domain of that particular specialization. And as we fulfill the territory of human permission, perhaps this is exactly what is needed to open up the next level of permission. Thus many missions will a new permission make. The permission that you choose to make for yourself in the time of your life is ultimately up to you.

Finally, a more advanced thought: what if the requirement upon the human race is to make something of the permission already granted before a new permission is given? Just as a mother will give a child a smaller portion of food, until she is satisfied that it can handle the helping already on its plate and is ready to try a larger portion. Perhaps the universe is waiting for us to venture into the unknown, to make it known and established, winning further bands of permission within the already established known domain and thus providing the foundations for a new appearance—a greater permission within which the human may safely explore further domains of universal power here on this planet.

We can see the appearance of an interconnected chain of permissions in the natural world. Take as an example a tree. A tree grows and naturally fills out its established domain. As it does so, it provides food and shelter, thus becoming joined by other life forms within the planetary chain of permissions.

Are we not ourselves another link in the already established chain of permissions?

The Language Soliloquy
A Lament

I have been alive for thousands of years. Since my birthplace in Egypt, I have multiplied and diversified, to have many expressions and styles, all over the world. Every human on the planet uses me and I am glad to be used. However, like everything on Earth, I want to grow and refine. When my high end is used, I rejoice; when my low end is used, I despair, for this is the part I wish to leave behind. But most of all, I need to expand and develop and open up new territories, connections and usage. I cannot do this on my own, I can only achieve new breakthroughs through the human. I have neither lungs nor larynx, voice box, tongue nor pen, ink or paper. It is for the human to pay back for the gift of language and speech and to push back my limitations, thus opening up new realms, and to discover that what you know of me is very small indeed and that I have great richness to offer to those who venture forth, not satisfied with established phrases and the constrictions of schoolbook grammar and syntax. If we had listened to established norms and never dared split an infinitive, we would not have the phrase "to boldly go where no human has gone before."

So, hear my lament, oh human, and respond, if you will, and you will be rewarded with great richness and discovery. Revelation and new understanding can be thine, providing you rest not until you find new means and ways of expression, and above all, new value, meaning and depth to the words and language you think you already know so well.

Fear

To begin with, fear is an override function which takes a person out of what they are doing and mobilizes them into action, often without the involvement of their conscious decision-making mechanisms. How many people are alive today only because at some time in their life fear had taken over, calling their instinct into action and at the last minute causing them to avoid an oncoming car or truck by instantly getting them out of the way of danger? This fear has one purpose only—to preserve life and maintain health and well being. It has the power to recruit physical attendees and helpers to cause a person to move faster; it works in partnership with the moving center energies and can mobilize into action your adrenalin glands, the heart, eyes, the kidneys and the sweat glands.

The human has an innate fear of the unknown. Knowing this, a person can help a child, for example, get over their fear of the dark by keeping a small night light burning in its bedroom. Some adults might also find easement from this simple remedy. For once the eyes can see and the brain can interpret what it sees, the shadows cease being monsters and once again become shadows attributed to familiar objects and a person can put recognition with what they had been previously hearing or seeing in the dark. Thus fear is often caused by lack of information and "being in the dark" about anything can cause fear. Even the worst news can be handled better and dealt with when it is known; it is the not knowing and the speculation of what might happen that causes the greatest fear. Thus sometimes it is useful to ask, in a fearful situation, "What is the worst scenario that can happen in this instance?"

Perhaps the greatest fear is the fear of death, but it is only fearful because we do not know what awaits us 'on the other side.' People who firmly believe in life after death are often not afraid at this time of change and may even welcome death as a relief from suffering and pain.

Fear is a very immediate emotion in that it causes rapid physiological changes. This has been exploited by writers, movie-makers and media people to make money, for humans seem to enjoy being scared in safe circumstances, when they know it is really "all right," for it is only make-belief really. This strange combination of knowing and not knowing must, however, cause a contradiction in the system which thus instructed might learn to distrust the confused signals it is getting from the human eyes and brain.

Some fears are not really fears at all and could come under the description of timid, uncertain or shy. These are born of a weak assembly and the fact that a person is unsure of themselves and what they are doing. For who is timid when a building is on fire and they need to interrupt an important conference to shout "Fire" and thus save lives? This kind of fear stems from how a person thinks about themselves, their importance and their purpose.

There are also fears which are groundless but somehow affect a person deeply. These might go back to childhood ignorance and can only be dealt with by applying reason and a decision making process. They will not go away over night, but if you make a list of what they are, you can slowly begin to deal with them by firstly deciding that they are irrational and you do not want to be subject to them any longer, and secondly by trying to find out why you are affected in the first place. Thus the reasoning process begins to take over from the emotional response and eventually, when the fear comes up again, you will have a rationale to put in its place.

The fear that keeps a person succeeding is one they can

To My Soul and to Me

Let this life not be wasted. Give me the strength and vision to be constant in my endeavor and open to new ways. Let not old patterns and habits cloud my sight and take away from the short time left to me.

May this great adventure continue. Continuance is the greatest gift given to me, for within it I can write upon the clean sheet of my life and add to the untold story. May wisdom guide my every move, in partnership with a daring and a courage, for we are stepping into the unknown, which beckons from behind the veil. I know it and feel it and every cell tingles with excitement at the thought of what is possible and awaits, still unwritten.

So give me the strength to step boldly into the future and to find ways to become a conduit for God and this new fresh essence that speaks to me of its longing to be born.

Stories from the Past

Experience of a London Bombing

It was September 1975. I was standing in the foyer of the Hilton Hotel in London, making a phone call from one of their soundproof booths, when a bomb detonated in the middle of the lobby. My back was to the explosion and the sound was muffled where I stood, so I did not know what was happening and I thought it was something wrong with the phone, as I could see sparks flying and my connection went dead. My left arm was resting on a ledge where I had placed my bag and at first I did not even realize that I was hurt. As I slowly turned around I could see a small fire in the middle of the lobby, someone was lying on the floor and a man was running towards me. As he escorted me out of the building, I began to realize that I must have been injured. I could hardly breathe and all I could think of at that moment was my next breath.

I had gone into the Hilton Hotel at Hyde Park Corner to make a phone call. I had taken a bus from the apartment where I was living at the time above an antique shop in the King's Road. It was the last day of my holidays and I was due to return to work at the Performing Right Society in the West End the next day. I was enjoying this last day of leisure, having safely escorted my son Peter to an English school, which was a new experience for him. After a year of establishing myself in Britain, in a new job and applying for a British passport, I had at last been able to bring my son to live with me in my new country. I had just returned to England from Poland, where I grew up and where my son was born. Three days earlier I had arrived at Victoria station, explaining to the five-year-old boy that he would need to learn a new language, as not many people in London spoke Polish. We caught a taxi from the station to the apartment and on the way I was explaining to him that he would not be understood, when the taxi driver turned around and started speaking fluent Polish to us.

On the previous day Peter had gone to school for the first time in his young life and he began by learning English in a special class for foreign students. He had been quite upset that he was not in class with the other children and again, I explained to him that he needed to learn the language first before he could rejoin the regular lessons. So on this particular day I had taken him to school and was on my way to meet a girlfriend for lunch. I had tried to phone her at work from the phone booths at Sloane Square, but they were all either taken or not in use. In the meantime a bus came along and I jumped aboard, planning to phone from the Hilton Hotel, where I knew there were several public telephones in the lobby.

So there I was, escorted to an ambulance, which was taking a number of the people from the hotel who were injured to the nearby hospital of St. Michael's which at the time was located at Hyde Park Corner. I learned later that my arm was badly hurt and I was very lucky that there was a visiting surgeon from Australia who specialized in skin grafts, for I needed both bone and skin transplants. The doctors debated whether to amputate my arm or not, but decided to perform the necessary operations to save it, because the nerve connections were intact and I still responded to sensations in my left hand. So six operations later, I now have skin from my abdominal area on my arm and skin from my leg patching up my abdomen. I have a piece of my left hip bone inserted into my lower arm as well as a metal plate. However, I feel whole and I am grateful to have two working arms and two legs, even *if one limb is somewhat disfigured. I feel very grateful to be alive, for if I had stood a few inches further left, it could have been my head that was hit, not my arm.*

I took several lessons from that experience. One is that anything can happen any time, and no matter how well you are prepared or think you are prepared for life's offerings, there are always surprises—both good and bad. And even the "bad" ones have good lessons to offer, because difficult experiences are character forming and strengthening. I believe that those who have been through life's turmoils and tribulations are better equipped to extend a helping hand to others in need.

A few weeks later, when I was still in hospital, one evening news came over the radio that there was another bombing nearby, at Green Park. I was very moved to watch dozens of doctors and nurses streaming back into the hospital, because they had heard the news on their way home and had turned around to come back to St. Michael's to offer their professional help, in case it was needed. Luckily not many people were hurt in that bombing. But the feeling of community, solidarity and humanity constituted a very healing presence in hospital that night.

When in hospital I wrote the following words:

There is a Pain

There is a pain beyond which there is no pain
There is a fear beyond which there is no fear
There is a belief beyond which there are no doubts
And I will have the strength to reach it.

The IRA (Irish Republican Army) claimed responsibility for the bombing in the Hilton Hotel that day. After the incident, when this fact became known, people would ask me, "Aren't you angry?" or "Don't you want revenge?" or "Doesn't it make you feel bitter?" My reply to them was, no, I do not want to take anger or bitterness or hate into my life. People who plant bombs do so out of hate. If my response was hate, then I would become like them, taking the very disease they suffer from into myself. People who feel hatred and harm others will need to live with the fact that their life is about hate and anger. My life is not about hate and anger; it is about forgiveness and learning and helping others. How can I improve if I want revenge? I am not responsible for other people's lives, but I am responsible for mine. So today I feel that if I can pass on this one lesson that I have learned, then I will have made good use of the experience on that fateful day, difficult as it was at the time.

As for my son, some good and generous people that I worked with took care of him and by the end of six weeks, when I came out of hospital, he spoke English quite well!

Jadwiga

This story takes place in Poland in the early fifties.

Jadwiga had been a young girl of seven when she was first introduced into our classroom. She was taciturn and shy; she was dirty and unkempt. Obviously neglected, she never had the right books or crayons or compass for each lesson. The other children whispered amongst themselves that she was the daughter of an alcoholic, though most of us did not understand what this meant. Certainly no one in that classroom could imagine what terrors she had had to endure to become so withdrawn and reluctant to communicate. All we children could see was a sloppy, untidy girl with dirty ribbons in her hair, who was never prepared for the lessons and never had the latest fashionable color of stockings or blouse under the compulsory school uniform smock.

This was her second year at school; during the first year she had always occupied a double school bench all by herself, as no one wanted to sit next to her and the teachers had not insisted that this avoidance of ours be rectified or changed. However, this year I had decided to take my place next to her and I sat with her lesson after lesson, still unable to communicate or to win her trust. Withdrawn and shy, she kept herself to herself, disappearing immediately after the last bell sounded, heralding the end of the school day, still unable to talk with anyone at the school.

On this particular fall day each row was assigned an exercise to do during our math lesson and for Jadwiga to complete the exercise she was given, along with the row she was in, required the use of a ruler. Jadwiga did not have a ruler and she looked around for one in vain. She finally asked me if I had one, but I had not brought one to school either, so I could not help her on this occasion. In front of Jadwiga sat another girl, Alicja, who always had the right equipment, kept in a neat wooden pencil box with a sliding lid. Inside was a brand new wooden ruler, alongside a compass, a couple of pencils and an eraser. Jadwiga tapped the girl on the shoulder and in a timid, quiet voice asked whether she could borrow this girl's ruler. Alicja turned around and looked condescendingly at Jadwiga.

"No, you can't have it," she said with annoyance in her voice. Perhaps it was surprising that an eight year old girl could look at another girl with such superiority and contempt, but she did. Alicja was the type of girl who had neatly braided hair, freshly pressed clothes, sandwiches wrapped up in neat packages made of brown paper and the right answers to most of the questions the teachers posed when they were checking the previous lesson's homework.

I saw this happen and wondered what I could do to help. I knew that the girl sitting in front of Jadwiga would not respond to my pleas or requests or even threats. There was such a self-righteous air about her that I knew persuasion would not work. There must be another way, I thought. And then something happened, for I found myself saying out loud, so that both Jadwiga and the girl sitting in front of us could hear: "If I had a ruler I would let you have mine, but I haven't got one." Somehow by some miracle, this seemed to work, for suddenly Alicja turned around, with her ruler in hand and quietly placed it onto Jadwiga's side of the desk in front of her.

"There you go," she whispered, as if ashamed and chastised, "you can have it."

Knowing the Name of the Enemy

In 1949 when I was six, my father, a Polish Jew and a physicist who had collaborated with Albert Einstein (they had written "The Evolution of Physics" together) was invited by the Polish government to return to his native country from Canada, where he had been working as a Professor at the University of Toronto throughout the Second World War. He was offered the opportunity to help build a Theoretical Physics Institute at Warsaw University, and he saw this as an exciting challenge. He decided to check out the situation "on the ground" before moving permanently back to Poland and sending for his wife, my mother, and his two children—my brother and me.

One year later in the summer of 1950 after my father had decided that he wanted to continue his work in Warsaw and that it was safe for us to join him, we packed up our belongings and sailed across the ocean to Poland, which was still devastated after the war. Warsaw (which by anagram saw war) was still mostly in ruins, though new districts and streets were mushrooming out of the rubble with a spirit of indomitability and hope. Soon after arrival, with the beginning of the academic year in September, we were sent to school and very slowly started to learn the new and difficult language. A few months into this new situation, as I began to settle into my new country, my parents, who knew that I loved to dance, enrolled me at the State Ballet School. I passed the entrance exam and was beginning to adjust to this new scenario when I contracted TB and was consequently sent to a sanatorium in the mountains of Slovakia (then part of Czechoslovakia), where I was confronted with new surroundings, a new language and many new faces. Away from home for six months, I began to adjust and learn yet another language—Slovakian. My mother managed to come and visit me once during this time, and my only connection to family was through letters, which were few and far between. It was a tedious time for a lively child of seven, left mostly to my own devices with a lot of spare time and not much to do. I remember the high point of the day was when an orderly came around every afternoon and brought us each an apple (I guess they believed that "an apple a day" helped the doctors do their job better); we cherished that fruit and ate it slowly, enjoying every part of it, except the stem. I befriended the girl in the next bed and we developed a competition to see who had more apple pips that day, laying them out on our bedside tables for the other to see, and comparing numbers.

It was at this time that the feelings of betrayal and abandonment came up in me time and again, probably because I did not understand well enough why I needed to be there, away from my family and everything I had been growing accustomed to in my new country.

When at last I returned home I had lost my English and the little bit of Polish I had acquired before being sent to the sanatorium, and I was speaking only Slovakian, which no one around me could understand. I had lost my place in the ballet school, as the children in my class had moved on in their dance skills, so that it would have been impossible for me to catch up with them, unless I was prepared to lose a year and start all over again. So the decision was made for me to return to my old classroom, where I remained for the rest of my school years.

Throughout the years the feeling of abandonment continued to surface from time to time when for whatever reason—real or imaginary—I thought I was being left *out or forgotten, or someone had missed me out when inviting their friends to a party or an outing.*

Years later, when I was married and grown up, I would still sometimes fall prey to this feeling of being missed out, forgotten and unloved. It was not until my husband pointed out to me one day that I was "wearing my sanatorium face" that I was able to laugh it off and recognize it for what it was, whenever it threatened to reappear. "Wearing my sanatorium face" became a code phrase for this feeling of self-pity and so I now had a name for this unwanted emotion, a handle with which I could control it. It made me think of the story of Rumpelstilskin—to have the name of something allows one to take control and make informed decisions about whatever it is that we are confronted with. For example, if you are not feeling well, you might justifiably worry about your health, but the moment someone competent, like a doctor, gives your condition a name, you know what you need to do and can take it on, like launching a campaign, no matter how serious the condition and how tenuous the prognosis. Thus I no longer wear my "sanatorium face" for long, because when I am in danger of doing so, I remember Rumpelstilskin and am able to laugh at myself.

In Pursuit of Development

Red and White Revival

The history of the red and white peoples living on this land is painful and fraught with injustice, exploitation and lack of understanding. Both races could harbor regret, anger and bitterness on the one hand and guilt and shame with a continued misrepresentation of history on the other. We could claim responsibility for the deeds of our ancestors and feel antagonism towards each other. There is a lot of healing that needs to go on, but if we don't start now, we never will and the chasm between us will keep growing. Neither the white man nor the red man is going to go away and both can learn from each other. The red man has a history and a spiritual tradition rich in content and planetary connection; the white man brings with him the history of European culture, art and literature, representing the high and the low, the good, the bad and the curious.

Neither one owns the land, whatever their claims may be. Neither are original people, for both came from somewhere and there was a time when this land was uninhabited by either. The "native" people were here before the white man ever knew America existed and thus have an earlier claim. Both the red and the white men are mortal and are but temporary visitors here.

Perhaps now, in looking to the future, there can be a red and white revival, marked by respect for and connection to the blue of the planet which can bring a healing and a new way. Thus, rather than facing each other in an antagonistic and competitive way, as the red and white have done on numerous occasions throughout history,* there can be a mutual concern and purpose, for the planet needs our help and our rescue.

* *The War of the Roses*
* *The Cold War, symbolized on either side by the red star of Russia and China and the white star of the USA.*

value

If you can find value for the little things in life, every moment can become a richness and a joy. "You only get out of life what you put into it" is so true and it is never too late to start putting in more. There is value in being able to feed one's body from day to day, to have the health and strength to walk down the street, to have the time to enjoy a conversation with a friend or to learn something new.

Question: Why is something valuable?

1. Does rarity cause something to be valuable?
Why are rubies more valuable than pebbles? Is it because they are rare or because they shine? A rare stamp, even if misprinted, becomes valuable; so does a rare jewel.

How does the planet view rarity? Is the air less valuable because there is an abundance of it and it is free? How would you feel about air if it was taken away?

2. The price tag.
Do people value what they get for free? What if we had to pay for air, language, feelings, emotion, love? Do we save it and use it wisely or do we squander it without much thought or appreciation? What is the real price of anything?

There are three kinds of payment we make for what we get: money, energy and time.

Do you value your body and faculties? If so, which parts? What about those that are unseen or that you don't even know about? How does that value manifest? Are there parts of you that you do not value because you don't like them (for whatever reason)? If we don't like a part of our body, we deprive it of its due appreciation and love, and thereby it is more likely to become diseased.

3. Following the lead.
If everyone else thinks something is valuable, will you follow their lead and assume they are right? How many times have you adopted something into your life, even if you didn't really want it or like it, because others persuaded you or you saw that they thought it was of value? The whole raison d'être of fashion is based in this assumption that others know best what to wear.

4. If you lose something, do you value it more?
An obvious example is your health or your freedom, but what about those parts of you that serve you well all the days of your life? Will you have to wait until you lose them to value them?

5. Do you value people or things because of what they can do for you?
Or do you value people and things simply because they exist and, like you, are part of Creation?

6. What you cannot do without.
Add up what these things are (for example, your faculties, food, the planet, the laws of nature…) and add up your value for them. Don't wait until they get taken away or you are in danger of losing them, but build into these

aspects of your life a permanent value so that you know where your value lives and you can reach out for it any time, any place, if you need it. For example, contemplate for a moment what it would be like to not be able to sleep or not be able to die, to add up your value for these natural processes.

7. Have a value added life.
Realize that by valuing something you add value to it. Do you know that when you value something, you add your power to it so that it sparkles and shines and thus can be valued even more? An easy to see example is when you decide you want something that has been in the store for a long time, but when you bring your money to pay for it, someone has just bought it. By deciding you wanted it, you had added value to it and made it more attractive to others.

Value what you have and it will become more valuable. If you value your life and existence, they will become more valuable and others will come to value you more, as well.

8. Are you of value? Will you be of value to something higher than you? How valuable are you to your family, your community, your country or to the planet itself?

9. What will your surrender value be?

What Makes Something Valuable?

Is it because it happens to be rare?
Or is it because others stop, admire and stare?
Is it because it has a high price?
Or is it because we think it is nice?

And can how we think cause the value to soar?
By taking it away, do we value it more?
Is it because of what it can do—
Can this cause something to be precious to you?

Is it because you need it to live?
Or is it because of the gifts it will give?
Is the criteria for value outside or in?
And thinking of creational value, where to begin?

The Value of Food

There once was a wise man who had a lot of value in his life. He valued the simple things and never wanted more than he needed at the time.

One day, a lady came to visit him and help him in his work. She also offered to do his shopping for him and on her return from the stores, as she was putting the food into the fridge, she noticed how appetizing everything looked and it made her feel hungry. So she turned to the man and asked him why the food in his fridge looked so fresh and good and inviting, more than the food this lady had bought for herself, even though she shopped at the same store and, in fact, had some identical items in her own fridge. The man's food looked more appetizing than any food she had ever seen in her life.

"It's simple," the man replied. "We value our food more and therefore it looks tastier. We make it better by how we think about it."

Have you noticed how mama's food tastes best? Is this perhaps because of the value and care she puts into it, rather than the ingredients or recipes she uses?

Clairvoyance

When you look at something, you see it. You see it from your perspective, you see it with your own bias, education, likes and dislikes, but you see it and nobody disputes that you do. You trust your own eyes because you have had physical proof to confirm that what you have seen is really there.

With clairvoyance, results are not immediately seen or perceived. The word itself means "clear sight" and refers to the ability (which everyone has) to perceive the unseen, to detect frequency and simply know what lies beyond the material manifestation of something. So, clairvoyance is, for example, knowing what another person is thinking or feeling, knowing what will happen next, predicting the future, as well as reading the past.

Each person carries their history around with them in the form of electro-magnetic signals which are registered inside their aura. When your clairvoyant faculty switches on, you can know about another person without asking; you will sense and read their history, as well as their current thoughts and feelings. And just as each person carries around their history inside their aura, so does every building, place, site, street, district and country have an astral light that is full of history, radiations, essences and influences.

For why do people in different parts of the world speak with different accents? Language is the LAND-GUAGE and represents a read-out of the essences of the land. Thus, for example, people from the Southern States who speak with a southern drawl process a different kind of energy than, say, a New Yorker. Their speeds will be different and their way of thinking will be different, their behavior will be different as well. Try to speak slowly to a Northener and they will most probably become impatient. Try adopting a California attitude in Boston and see how far you get with it.

Clairvoyance is the ability to detect what radiation goes with what, to recognize the features of a land or place without previous knowledge or research. It is the ability to arrive in a country and to simply know what the prevailing energies of that part of the world are, so as to be able to adapt to the change of frequency and radiation and to successfully communicate with the natives, without superimposing one's own customs or habits (it is a little more difficult to change one's accent).

Imagine going to the Taj Mahal or walking into a room and knowing its history, as well as being able to pick up, like a receiving station, what had gone on in it in the last few hours or days or even longer. Perhaps one would then also be able to heal an atmosphere and even out the ups and downs that might occur in a place in the course of a normal working day. Or one could detect a presence and help exorcise a bad feeling that lingers after an argument in a room or home, or even send a ghost back to where he or she had come from.

If people could learn clairvoyance as part of a natural education, the world would be a much more peaceful place, for we would understand each other better, rather than trying to enforce our own ways and customs on others who have different beliefs and traditions. We would know that each person is moved by a different set of essences and energies and so, rather than judging another for being different, we might welcome the variety and change as a learning opportunity.

Every Moment Counts

There is something everyone agrees upon, as they get older — the older you get, the faster time seems to fly. The seasons and the years do not linger long and before you know it, another birthday has added another unit to your age.

Isn't it strange, how there is an ongoing guessing game, how old everyone you meet is. We tend to describe people, even to ourselves, in terms of their age, whereas this is the most impermanent description you could possibly think of. And as we grow older, policemen, doctors and other professionals with whom we deal, seem to get younger and younger. Have you noticed how young the Olympic athletes are this year? "No," someone might say, "you are getting older." Well, so are you my friend. And as time flies by, as there is less and less of it left, it becomes so much more precious. If we knew the time and date of our departure (death), would that alter our behavior? We all know our birthday. Who celebrates their death-day? But looking at it another way, perhaps our death is really our birth into something new, and by far a greater reason to celebrate than our birthday.

There is the possibility that time is speeding up, for even younger people these days are noticing the accelerated passage of time, even those who used to think they had all the time in the world. Perhaps there is a new urgency abroad, a knowing that these moments we now have will never be ours again to squander or savor, depending on our inclination and choice.

If you know what you want in this life, perhaps there is still time to achieve it. If you don't, then how can anything or anyone help you, how can you make decisions about how you are going to spend your time, the most precious commodity that you have? Never mind silver and gold, riches and jewels; time will allow you to achieve all that, if that is what you want, and more. Without it, we have come to the end of our journey and there is no more for us to do or be or achieve.

Spend your time wisely. Learn now not to suffer fools gladly or waste time, to speak your mind and go for what you want, thus living the wisdom of old age today. Most people learn these things when it is already too late. So, how much time do you have left? No one knows, not even you. Whatever the answer, it is not much and you have probably used up over a quarter of it already. Look back for a moment to see how you have spent your time thus far and from that knowledge, make a decision whether you want your future to be different. If so, start now and set your feet upon the path of change, to begin to take control of your life, your time, your now, for THIS IS THE TIME OF YOUR LIFE.

As the sands of your time sift through the hourglass of your life, can you afford to waste one grain or lose your sense of value and appreciation for every single moment that is still left?

Outside the Church

Standing outside the church I hear the singing, as it carries through the cold winter air. The words are ancient, in celebration of a man and an event that occurred on this planet two thousand years ago.

I am standing outside the church but I am standing inside the church of nature—open and available to all, where new sermons are broadcast every day for all to hear and understand. This is the most accessible church where I will never feel like an outsider or a stranger.

I look around me and everything speaks to me. The very fact of winter is a promise of the spring yet to come. The cold causes preservation and thus the winter is a time for dwelling upon those things one would want to uphold, keep and hang on to. High force is accompanied by cold temperatures and thus I wonder what high force is coming into this part of the planet at this time of year.

I look up and see the stars; I sense a feeling of awe and wonder and there is a humility and understanding that there is so much more to experience, to comprehend, to reach out towards. Will this lifetime be sufficient to gather the information I need and collect the force necessary to make the journey home?

I feel a surge and power rise in me. There is support for life here and everything encourages me to go on. Every small victory is an achievement recognized by some greater power that can only be hinted at and sensed, which must be made up of many tiny working parts, just as each cell in the body contributes to the well being and ongoing health of the whole.

So Many

So many people have been born onto planet Earth. So many have tried to make a difference and so many wanted to leave their mark and wanted to be remembered for the works that they had done.

Where are they now? They have left behind them works of art, great writings and thoughts, ideas, contemplations and prayers. All the great people of the past had something in common—they were not too concerned about their own personal comfort or safety; they had a greater purpose to fulfill which had taken them out of the repetition of the ordinary into the unusual, the better, the new.

These are demanding and allowing times, for rather than follow the examples handed down throughout history, packaged by each new generation, we have the permission to express and create our own new ideas and writings and ceremonies and means and ways. As long as they are based in what is real and what is newly appearing on this planet today, they will have potency, connection and effect, in ways unheard of in the corridors of history or the chambers of the currently available references and understandings.

The book of life is yet to be written; it waits.

Aging

Growing up, maturing and aging are all aspects of the same process but the human attitude to each is different, the evidence of which is the fact of having three separate words within the language for this ongoing process. At which point does one end and another begin?

Change

There is a known saying, that the only constant in our lives is change. And yet the human seeks stability and constancy on the one hand, while he or she is drawn to the new and is urged towards improvement on the other. Our lives are a continuous adjustment to reconcile change with habit and established patterns.

In looking at nature, her cycles are constant, in that the spring follows winter and summer follows spring. We have come to rely on this sequence of events and indeed our livelihoods depend on this regularity. However, the patterns it follows are constantly changing in that no two summers are the same and every fall brings with it a new palette of color and a unique theatrical display of light, shade and hue. This originality gives us endless topics of conversations, to the point where weather, the seasons, the temperature are probably the most talked about subjects on planet Earth.

If we had a longer view and could see the seasons in terms of thousands, or even millions of years, rather than the few decades we might have experienced within our lifetime, we would probably be astonished at the multiple changes in our world—we would witness ice ages, continental shifts and multiple polarity changes; we would see earthquakes and volcanic eruptions that have changed the cartographic profile of the planet we live in. Alongside planetary developments, we would also witness the coming and going of species and the evolution of the human kind.

Even in our lifetime, the map has changed several times already and these days regular replacements are probably included in an annual school budget. Therefore we should not be surprised that our own make-up shifts with the sands of time and that imperceptibly, day by day, we are changing and altering to the point where major adjustments might be needed to abruptly adjust to our new constantly emerging circumstance. Thus a change might seem sudden at the time but it probably had a long history of arriving. This can happen at either end of the scale—as an improvement or a degeneration. A serious disease is most often the result of a worsening condition over a long period of time and when looking back, very often the warning signs could have been detected long ago, but no one knew how to or wanted to. We tend to ignore what we do not want to know.

Likewise, a regenerating change has its history too and if a person works hard at something day by day by day, the result of this work will change and alter them, so that they will become an expert or a master or an authority in their chosen field. There is a saying, "Practice makes perfect;" as perfection does not leave room for improvement, perhaps it should be, "Practice makes better" instead.

There are over six billion people in the world and as they are all changing all the time, tomorrow there will be over six billion different people in the world and the day after tomorrow, a new set of six billion plus will emerge from slumber alongside those that will enter planet Earth and be born. All our billions of parts are changing day by day as well. Which way are they going?

God's Designers
Series

God's Designers Series

The purpose of this series is to take a refreshing and sometimes humorous look at the design and workings of ourselves and our surroundings, with a reference to value, appreciation and gratitude.

Imagine for a moment what it would be like to have been God's designer, to be given the task of designing a tree, a hand, or even an entire human being. The task would have been beyond us. Perhaps we have been sent to this planet to be re-educated, because we have failed as God's designers. Or perhaps we are God's designers in training, with the opportunity to earn this coveted position.

In this series we present a few ideas of what God's designers might have had to contend with, if God had been willing to delegate these tasks to someone of an intelligence which is inferior to His/Her/Its own, but perhaps with a potential to even become equal.

The Human

The human was the most difficult and complex task any of God's designers had to face. So intricately balanced with all the millions of parts working together in unison, so self sufficient on the one hand and so beautifully integrated with its environment and ecology on the other.

Able to feed itself and find and invent all the necessary tools to further promote its existence, with room for evolutionary development and growth, with a mind capable of reaching beyond the planet and even all the way up to God.

This was a daunting task and there really was no one capable of taking on the job of designing the crowning jewel of God's handiwork, except God Him/Her/Itself.

The Voice

There was a lot of excitement when the human was given a voice. This was no warble, not a bird song, a howl, a grunt, a roar, a bark or a hiss. It was nothing like anything that had hitherto been heard from any animal and certainly could not be compared to the majestic sounds of nature. The range was at first unbelievable—how could one small voice box located in the throat and moderated by the use of tongue, lips and breath produce such a huge range and variety of sounds? The very implications of this and the anticipated possibility of language and inter-human communications were so far reaching that it seemed impossible for the human to ever become victim to misunderstandings or lack of comprehension.

The clarity of the voice, the melodic span of octave and note, the subtlety of nuances and half-notes, the moderation of color and the modulation of musical expression seemed to assure and guarantee that the human would never be without music. These gifts were enormous and generous on behalf of God, bringing the human closer to being godlike himself. God's designers marveled at God's ingenuity and wondered at the many imaginative uses the human could begin to put this precious gift towards. Speculations were made as to the range and variety of musical sounds and notes that would undoubtedly fill the air of the fair planet the human was given as its home. There was the appreciation that music would surely be everywhere and the sweet sounds of melodic harmonies would soon fill the atmosphere as the human would no doubt experiment with its newfound gift and discover new ways of expressing its feelings and longings and above all, its gratitude towards God.

When it was understood that the many sounds produced by the human throat and mouth could be organized in such a way as to make a series of unique and meaningful sounds that could be sequenced into a system of words, sentences, concepts and understandings that would express the gamut of human thoughts, revelations and discoveries, there was an awe-struck silence as God's designers tried in vain to master the inter-relationships of words, grammar, syntax, sentences and speech. It was truly a marvel when it was realized that this would be a free gift, passed on from generation to generation to be used by the human at will, to be refined and developed as the human would begin to fulfill its design.

When it was understood that the human would have the capability of learning the skill of language and speech within three years or less from the moment of birth, from then on to be able to apply it to any situation, meaning or feeling, it became clear that communication was an important ingredient within the human journey of self discovery. This gift was destined to become a tool of learning and connection, freely given and available to all, to be used freely and abundantly as the human saw fit to further its journey of life on planet Earth.

It was a rich experience to begin to think how the human could utilize this gift and how the millions of expressions could be put together to give credence to the great wealth of the surroundings the human found itself in, to find ways of communicating its feelings and how language could become a mutual reminder as to the purposes of life, Creation and the human's short sojourn on planet Earth.

There were visions of poetry and connective language as the human now had the wherewithal to write its own prayers, devotions, meditations and contemplations. There were enough ways of stringing sounds and meanings together for each human to find its unique and original expression, different from all others and with the potential of reaching any destination within the known and unknown universe. The hidden attribute of language was that it could travel where it was sent to and at the same time carry the frequency of the sender, so that each phrase or expression, in finding its destination, could take with it a little bit of the frequency of the person that created it. Thus the human was being taught the subtle ways in which to imitate God and to find new ways to reach Him/Her/It.

Feet

We really laughed when God said He wanted the human to walk upright and He wanted us to design two platforms which would connect the human to the ground and would be able to move so that the human could get around in search of food and sustenance. He did not want these contraptions to be large and unwieldy and we could not imagine how such a large weight and tall construction as the human design could be supported and carried around on two small suction pads. They also needed to have a certain amount of grip and bend so that as they moved, such a small surface would be well attached to the Mother. We laughed and said, "Surely he will fall over!" But God assured us that the human would even be able to stand on its toes, to make himself seem taller than he already was if he needed, for example, to reach for something higher up.

When the design was complete, we were absolutely certain that God had defied His own laws and suspended gravity and aerodynamics on the piece of land where the now completed human stood.

"A creature on two legs," we cried with delight, clapping our hands with glee, at the same time wondering why all of God's other walking creatures needed at least four, if not more.

The Eyes

A device needed to be found that could record the world around the human without altering it, by bringing the image through an opening (or two) into the brain where it could be translated into electrical signals. This needed to be done without touch, without movement, instantaneously, so that when a person woke up in the morning they could take in an image of their surroundings and have a relatively accurate reconstruction of reality in their head so that they could make decisions and progress according to need. The device needed to be accessible and presentable so that it did not ruin the composition of the face and the whole design, as it needed to be visible and active all the time during waking hours, taking in impressions, light, signals and pictures. It needed to be able to be switched off or covered up at night so that too many impressions coming in would not disturb the human's sleep.

Then there was the question of color, shape, dimension and perspective and the concern as to how to translate the reception of signals into messages, which could be stored by the brain. There was also the need to regulate the amount of light coming into the device, so that it would never be too much and therefore damaging on the one hand, but could be regulated to let in more when the surroundings were dark and needed to be seen with only a small source of light visible.

Finally there was also the worry that if there was a device that would let signals directly into the brain, how could one make sure it was a one-way transmitting system so that signals would not spill out of the brain into one's surrounding space? Or, if it was a two-way contraption, how to make it safe and limited so that the entire contents of the brain did not escape a human all at once?

When the first eye was produced, we all thought it was a toy. It was too perfect, too smooth, too round; it would need lubrication, often many times a minute, if it was to be able to go on working for many hours at a time. How on Earth could we get it to do that? Finally there was another suggestion that it could be the gateway for excreting the cooling lubricant of tears, meant to contribute to the evacuation of an emotional charge, both high and low (tears of joy, tears of despair, tears of grief).

When the design finally arrived and was completed, we realized that no two eyes are the same and that even the color changed from person to person and was varied according to the genetic of the human and the state of his or her electrical and physical health.

And what a revelation it was to discover the ingenuity of having two eyes to provide depth and dimension, as well as two aspects of electrics—receiving and transmitting!

The Ear

When God's Designer created the ears, we, the trainees laughed a lot. Why would anyone want to look straight ahead, but listen to the sides? we asked. It will only make the human dispersed, we argued. They will never be able to concentrate — they will be looking at one thing or one person and listening to another. Far better make them listen through their eyes, we suggested, pleased with ourselves that we had found a fitting solution. God's Designer was very stubborn about this and would not listen (God knows where his ears were at this point!). So he attached the ears to the two sides of the human head and again, we were amazed, for they did not close or open; they were always available to receive sound. How could that be? How come a human has control over what they see and can look away or close their eyes altogether, but have no control over the sound they receive, unless they cover their ears with their hands, which is a very dramatic gesture that at the same time disables the hands, rendering it impossible to do anything else with these extraordinary tools? Of course, a human could stuff things into his ears to stop the hearing, but then what if something came along that they might want to hear, what then? We felt sorry for the human who would not be able to select what they wanted to listen to, but God assured us that the human would indeed have a very selective hearing capability that would become known as selective hearing. We asked how that would be possible and God explained that this would occur deeper in the head, once the sound had penetrated into the brain, at which point the human would have pre-installed filter systems, built in according to his experience, beliefs, likes and dislikes, aims, targets, prejudices, biases and disciplines. Thus, we were told, the human would be able to shut off certain sounds, information and energy coming through the curiously shaped sound wave portholes.

Then the question arose about sleeping. For when the human sleeps, they close their eyes. What would they do about their ears? They would need to find a quiet space to sleep, came the answer, or indeed they would be kept awake, unless they had dulled their sensitivity to a point of being able to sleep in a noisy environment. As we had already been given an insight into the possible progression of human evolution and had had a glimpse of some of the human machinery that they would be producing at some point in the future, we hoped these inventions (and especially their various loud modes of transportation) would not come off the drawing boards too soon so that the poor human could get some sleep and rest before the age of advanced mechanical devices and big city noises ruined their sleep forever.

The Blood

God said to His designers: "Design me a liquid that will course through the body of this human, delivering oxygen, energy, nutriments and food to all parts, to every single cell. It should also be able to collect debris from the cells as well as carbon dioxide, to be safely deposited back into the lungs and expelled from the body, without contaminating the carrier itself.

"It needs to be balanced in such a way that it can be constantly replenished with new cells and ingredients which will be continuously manufactured within the depths of the bone marrow. It should also contain cells that are soldiers and servants of the white system, born and educated to attack and destroy unwanted invaders (of which the human will have many), then to be expelled from the body, together with the conquered intruders.

"In its journey toward all parts, it can take advantage of the fact of gravity, but on the return journey it needs to be able to defy gravity and find a way of efficiently traveling up and down the human arms and legs, and around their vital organs and through the central nervous system and up into the head and face.

"Clearly it will need a pump that will keep the blood regularly circulating round the human body all the days of its life—when awake, asleep, when active or at rest. This pump will need to be flexible so that it can adjust its speed to match the requirements of the moment—to pump faster when action or exertion are required, or when fear or instinct prepare the body for flight or fight; slower when the person is at peace or at rest in, say, a meditative state.

"It will need to have the correct mineral content with more iron for the men and more copper for the women—the mystery of gender should find its expression even at the level of the blood. Iron is governed by Mars and copper by Venus; thus these two influences will be held within the record of the blood.

"It should have the ability to heat up when needed, if fighting intruders on a larger scale, which shall be called 'having a fever,' or when in exertion; it should also be able to distribute heat to every cell of the body or, alternatively, to cool down every part when the outside temperature is high. There will be a limit to how much heat a person can take and process at any given time, and if they allow their blood to 'boil,' then they may bring upon themselves a dangerous condition, for, as the blood cools down, so it will use up a large amount of energy.

"And, although made up of many parts, most of which will be colorless, it will need to be red in order to effectively fulfill its function—bright red when oxygenated and traveling on its journey from the lungs through the heart to all parts of the body and a darker, more bluey red when returning to the heart to be sent back to the lungs, carrying carbon dioxide that needs to be passed out of the body into the alveoli of the lungs, through their thin walls which will allow gases, but not liquids to pass.

"And finally, there should be many charges that can be passed around the body within the blood. One of these charges needs to be genetic, so that the human bloodline is preserved from generation to generation. The way it needs to work is for the charge to course around the body until it reaches the brain, there to be played out in the unique combination of characteristics that everyone in the world inherits, forms and displays every moment of *every day—from gesture and posture to the tensions of the skin, the way of the walk, the smile, the frown, the dancing step, the voice, the language, the tilt of the head, the pronenesses, talents and acquired habits."*

At this point God's designers knew they were facing an enormous task and worked tirelessly day and night, trying to put together the liquid that would sustain life and purify itself in doing so. However, the greatest obstacle of all turned out to be the design of the pump, for although the team knew exactly what a pump should look like, they could not make one small enough to fit into the chest cavity where God wanted it to be located and they did not know how to protect it from being bruised, damaged or hurt. Above all they did not know how to design a trigger mechanism to keep it going, even while the human was asleep or thinking about other things.

So yet again God had to intervene to put it all together and make it work. The great secret of the tic-toc of the heart was to connect it up to the power grid of the planet, tune it to the same frequency and have it respond to the natural spark that runs through the human's earthly host. In explaining the mechanism of this device, God held up a single cell taken from a human heart as it continued to beat to the same rhythm as the entire heart muscle—baboom, baboom, baboom; every single human heart beating to its own unique rhythm. This was achieved by tuning the human heart to the Earth (heart even anagrams to Earth), by having it located within the chest cavity at exactly the same angle as the earth is angled within the solar system; its connection to the sun level electric spark was then assured by locating a minute amount of gold in the heart, which is the metal divinated to the sun.

The greatest wonder was to see how every aspect of the human design was totally unique and individual, tailor made to suit its host and yet at the same time the design itself is the same for all — effective and working, ready for action and life within which each person can find their own expression, thanks to the Creator who made them.

A Tree

I was asked to design a tree. Of course, I did not know what a tree was, for I had never seen one. In fact, trees did not yet exist, except as a concept in God's mind.

The task was to find a design that would alter shape between summer and winter. In summer it needed to be receptive and take in energy which it could then store and transmit into the ground. In the winter it needed to take on a transmissive, rod-like shape, so that energy could travel from the ground into the atmosphere. It needed to be able to live for a long time and survive these continuous changes year after year after year.

There needed to be a variety of shapes, sizes, qualities, frequencies to process different kinds of energy and produce a multiplicity of healing remedies. Some would need to bear fruit and be covered with colorful flowers in the springtime, others would need to produce nuts or cones, but they all needed to manufacture seeds in order to reproduce themselves and ensure continuance. Yet others would remain constant and green all year round. But all would need to grow tall and survive the human, thus bearing witness to their activities through several generations. They needed to be strong and flexible to successfully resist the power of the fall winds and in the cold north to bear the weight of winter snows. Some would need to withstand the heat of the sun all year round and others would need to survive the darkness of a sub-arctic winter.

The intricacy of the task was difficult enough, but my main stumbling block was the fact that my mind could not stretch to the idea of shedding leaves. I could not understand how a tree could grow an abundance of leaves in the springtime, which it would display all through the summer, only to drop them in the fall. It seemed such a waste to let so many delicate and beautifully designed green leaves dry up and fall down, only to be blown around by the wind, as if they had never been attached to their source of food. To my way of thinking, this was a great waste, because then, in the early spring, a whole new crop of leaves would have to be reproduced again, to be grown and developed by the tree from nothing, as if by magic.

God's chief designer then explained to me that the leaves would fall onto the ground and provide nourishment for the earth, which would thus become fertilized, to be able to provide new life in the springtime—grass, flowers and new trees, called saplings. I then realized that God's designer needed to think in terms of integration and harmony, not separation and individuality. I saw that God thinks in terms of all species and all heavenly bodies, for the trees take in energy from the universe—mainly from the sun (which is why the leaves and needles needed to be green, as they store the combined energies from the sun—yellow—and the Earth—blue), but also from other planets, from the moon, from its environment and even from the stars. Thus in the fall, when the tree no longer feeds the leaves with water (blue), they dry up and turn yellow, finally no longer even able to hold the dying energy of the sun (yellow).

This story explains why I have been sent here to Earth to learn further lessons on integration and how things can work in harmony and in inter-dependent chains of cause and effect.

A Mixed Bag

Comparison

What is little? What is large?

Is a matchbox little or large? Is a distant star great or small? Is an atom huge or miniscule? How tall is tall? Is someone taller than you tall and someone smaller that you small? How personal are your views of shape and dimension?

As we stand on our rung of a ladder stretching from nothing to infinity, so we view all else from that place. Looking down, we can view the worlds of microbes, atoms and sub-particles from our lofty heights; looking up, we can feel tiny and insignificant in view of the stars, Creation and God.

What if there was no gift of comparison and we stood alone, with nothing to measure ourselves against? What then? Would we feel great and important or small and insignificant? If we were smaller than an atom, or even an electron, would the worlds of particles appear to us to be as large as a universe and our solar system? Would we reconsider killing a bug if it was ten times greater than us?

For this lifetime we are physically trapped in a body and therefore will always be subject to its dimensions and needs, as well as its capabilities and limitations. But mentally we can inhabit the stars or shrink to become sensitized to the constituent parts of our blood or the DNA chains residing in our genes. Our ability to compare has allowed us to have understanding about ourselves and others and the world around us. However, if taken personally, it can become the walls of our prison and the limitation of our vision.

Our eyes look out through two small holes in the front of our head, looking always ahead, never back. We do, however, have other organs of sense and touch that with practice can detect what is happening in an area miles away. With training we can understand the small and the large worlds, but to do so a person would need to give up their unique point of view — it is unique because each person is of a different shape and dimension and if everything outside of them is seen in comparison to themselves, it will be awarded epitaphs that are not true to anyone else in the world. Thus we need to find universal laws and measuring devices that do not depend on personal interpretation but hold true in any part of the universe and within the micro-cosmos as well; laws that will apply, no matter what kind of body we might reincarnate into in the future (or in the past).

The moment we can see that we are not isolated and confined and not sentenced to being of the same dimension, shape, quality and consistency for ever and ever is the moment we can become liberated into being what we want to be. Thus a small man with charisma and belief in self can appear large and a large lady talking to a child with compassion and understanding can appear to be exactly as small or as big as the child.

Salad

This is a true story and challenges the reader's morality and sense of etiquette.
Note: Not for the squeamish.

There once was a rich woman who was very influential and had built up a large international company from scratch. She employed many people, most of whom respected her and some of whom feared her, as her power and bank account grew over the years. She was now past retirement age but continued to run the company with strict adherence to her principles of discipline, hard work and punctuality and to oversee its day to day processes and systems.

One day she invited two young executives—Andrew Smith and Anne Dawson—to her home for lunch. She intended to initiate a new important international project which could add world influence and renown to the company's already well respected name. The two executives had done well so far within the company, but if their careers were really to take off, this project could establish them firmly within the company's future and perhaps even secure a place on the board. The meeting was going to be held at her home, to follow a tradition of quiet executive gatherings where most successful projects had been born. She would dismiss the servants and make lunch herself in the kitchen so they could talk in peace and without interruptions. She would turn off the phone and intended to have a plan of action ready by the end of the allotted two hours. The time was set, it was agreed and on the day, at the appointed hour they rang the doorbell, briefcases in hand, full of anticipation and hope.

"Come on in," she said, motioning them inside as she opened the door. They walked into the large modern kitchen, all shiny and clean with white worktops and a white marble tiled floor.

"I didn't make a cooked lunch," she said, pointing to a large wooden bowl of crisp fresh salad which stood on a round white table in the middle of the kitchen floor. Next to it there was a round Camembert cheese on a small white marble plate and some French bread in a basket. The table was set for three and there were black linen napkins resting on three white plates. In fact, everything in the kitchen was either black or white, with black iron pans hanging in a row over the counter top.

"Is that all right?" she asked. "Do you like salad?"

"Oh, yes," they both replied enthusiastically as they sat down at the table. The older woman picked up the wooden salad serving fork and spoon set and began tossing the salad. Andrew was unfolding his napkin with meticulousness and attention, while Anne watched the salad being tossed—it looked so appetizing and fresh, and she was hungry, having dashed out of her house in the morning without having eaten anything for breakfast. Just at that moment she saw the older woman's jaw drop open and a small dribble escaped from her lips and fell into the middle of the salad. It was unnoticed by either of the others and very soon it was well mixed in with the dressing and the lettuce and tomatoes, cucumbers and onions. Anne watched transfixed, as she could no longer trace where in the salad bowl it was; no doubt it was by now everywhere, well mixed in and coating all the appetizing ingredients.

Her mind was racing—no one else had noticed, but she had and she knew. Should she mention something *and ruin the lunch or should she whisper something to Andrew and warn him not to eat the salad? How could they avoid it? They had both declared that they liked salad, there was not much else served and their future depended on the success of this lunch. They had worked so hard to prepare for it and in their briefcases they had a proposed agenda—their precious research, notes and plans. How could they possibly ruin it now?*

Challenge: What would you do?
Anne ended up eating the salad and never mentioning the story to anyone.

A Look at Human and World History
The Two Views

WHAT IS
I look at what is constant and has been like a thread of consistency through the ages.
WHAT CAN I DO?
I can be constant.

WHAT IS
The green grass and the blue sky were here when the first humans walked the Earth.
WHAT CAN I DO?
I can begin to put together a palette of color that has now transferred from nature and lives inside my head.

WHAT IS
Thus there is color, light, thus sound and voices, growth, the season, stars; day and night, dark and light. All this is subject to the laws.
WHAT CAN I DO?
I can put together a grid of the laws, starting with the Law of Duality.

WHAT IS
As a human I have a brain, a voice and an ability to reason.
WHAT CAN I DO?
What must I do to justify such gifts? Mere vegetation, existence, continuance are clearly not enough. These abilities are given me for a reason. They must be; I must always continue to try to find out what I am here to do.

WHAT IS
Vegetation is for the vegetation.
Existence is for flora and fauna.
What is the case for the human? Perhaps the potential of life immortal?
WHAT CAN I DO?
The human is higher. How high, is for me to discover. The only limitations are those I create for myself.

WHAT IS
Human life—humans have the rental license to inhabit multi-leveled equipment with the possibility and option to understand God's creation better than any other being has been able to understand up to this point.
WHAT CAN I DO?
Only time is the limit.

WHAT IS
There is a responsibility to take up the many talents and explore the depths to which a human faculty and mind can reach, embrace, penetrate; to open the hidden doors, find the secret keys and to express the compassion of God while alive here on Earth.
WHAT CAN I DO?
Nobody has yet discovered the limits of our capabilities. Perhaps there are none, only we might think there are.

WHAT IS
Every revelation is an invitation to continue along that particular path of reasoning. It is not an end to itself.
WHAT CAN I DO?
I must always look for the next revelation and the next inspiration, never settling to what has already been

achieved. Humans are satisfied with so little; it seems they are settled to merely survive another day, another month, another year.

WHAT IS
In being full of itself, water fills out every crack, every valley, every low place.
WHAT CAN I DO?
In being full, the human needs to express itself.

WHAT IS
We are like water, if we choose to fix ourselves at any particular level.
WHAT CAN I DO?
Expression leads to further understanding. We can instruct ourselves in the process, always seeking to find the next level.

WHAT IS—CONCLUSION
Therefore being satisfied should be a brief moment, else, like water that is stagnant, it turns into a blockage and prevents us from moving on.

Compassion

Compassion is the active ingredient in the ability to have an all-encompassing view in any situation, including one's view of oneself.

People have fragmentary views. If one fragmentary view looks at another, different fragmentary view, they will accuse each other of lack of compassion.

Real compassion is charged with the ions of connection to a higher purpose—elevation offers a larger view—thus it is not personally based. To see the full circumference of a circle, one must rise above it and thus cease to be influenced by its fragment, which can only be personal. The water, if its purpose is, for example, to clean, will have compassion, as it finds its level and has no bias as to who or what it cleans.

The human purpose is thus to be the best ghost imitation of the compassion of God that it can be, thereby becoming same-same with God and a true representative of the divine.

Meditation

1. THE HUMAN VIEW
Day and Night
a) It is day. The sun shines and all is bright, all is warm and all is glowing.
b) It is night. All is dark, cool, quiet, except for the nocturnal noises of animals.

The Four Seasons
a) Think of spring. The melting snow, fresh green growth, April showers, colorful flowers, the birds return and are nest building.
b) Summer. Vegetation in full bloom. Fresh vegetables, holidays. Warmth, the noises of summer.
c) Fall. The fall colors of orange, rust, yellow and red, falling leaves, the change in the weather. The rains, the mud, the fall flowers, the birds fly south.
d) Winter. The first snows, the shorter days, the cold. The white landscape, the silence.

2. THE PLANETARY VIEW
a) Try to image both day and night happening at the same

time, on different parts of the planet. See how the time of day rotates around the planet (as the planet rotates anti-clockwise, looking from north to south, so the time of day travels around the planet in an anti-clockwise direction). In other words, it is later the further east you go, until you hit the International Date Line and then you gain a day when traveling east and again start losing time the further east you go.

b) Try to imagine all four seasons happening on the planet at the same time: permanent winter at the North and South Poles and permanent summer at the equator. Fall and spring appear twice a year, once each on each hemisphere, traveling and spreading from the equator (spring) or from the poles (fall) — both at the same time. If you speeded up time, you would see the change of season as a change in coloring in the temperate zones — from green spreading from the equator (spring to summer), to browns and yellows appearing (from the north or south respectively), to white blanketing everything (winter), again, spreading from the poles towards the equator, but never reaching it. This shift in color is only in a comparatively narrow band within the northern and southern hemispheres.

3. THE SUN VIEW
Where I am, there is light and warmth all the time.

Thus, you can have a personal view, a planetary view or a solar view of yourself. The personal view is when you are subject to the law of opposites and you are either fast or slow, happy or sad, good or bad. The planetary view says that you are all those things in the course of a lifetime and therefore you are not subject to either *extreme, for you can always choose which it is going to be. The solar view says that your purpose here is to bring light and warmth into the world, and this tasking is not subject to the duality of a temporary mood or limitation.*

Presents or Presence?

The tradition of giving presents at Christmas is a comparatively recent addition to the folklore surrounding our festive customs and originates from the Victorian era.

The presents that are colorfully wrapped and placed under the Christmas tree are a physical manifestation of sentiment and endearment, a thought process that occurred in someone powerfully enough (for whatever reason) for them to act on it and make the effort to fulfill their intention. Then, usually on Christmas Day (though in some cultures it will take place on Christmas Eve), the great unwrapping of presents occurs and with it the receiver connects to the genuineness (or lack of it) of the intention of the giver and if he or she is sensitive enough, they will feel the radiation that comes with each gift, its wrapping, its card or label. Even the color of the wrapping tells a story.

Thus with a present comes a presence. A presence is the radiation of something that can be felt at distance from the object (or person) itself. For example, do they not say, "in the presence of Her Majesty the Queen"? The idea behind this statement is that royalty are those who have managed to establish a connection with a higher essence or entity or force and thus all who come near them should be able to feel that special emanation and influence. And thus to be in the presence of a person or a place that has, for example, healing properties and is connected to the healing force, it would be possible to become healed.

Therefore at Christmas people do not only give presents, but also the presence of themselves. For whoever you give your time to, you are offering the most valuable commodity you have, one that is always in short supply and one that money cannot buy. Thus pause for a moment this Christmas and consider what and who you give your presence to and why. Perhaps you will learn something about yourself!

The Greatest Present of All

As opposed to the past or the future, the present is the only time we have to do or think anything at all. We deceive ourselves if we think we have a future; we have only the next now and the next one and the next one. We deceive ourselves if we think we have a past; we have the residue of previous nows, which we can keep in the form of memories and experience.

The present can be seen as a gift from Creation, the only certainty we really have. This is the greatest gifting of all, for within it we can act, we can change, we can develop and learn. If it is used wisely, we can become the very qualities we process in our ever progressing nows, moment by moment. A person who continues to perform wise acts becomes wise; a person who performs courageous acts becomes courageous.

Thus who and what you are at this moment is the telling result of how you have used your greatest gift — the time of your life and the power of your now.

Speaking of Tongues

If you have seen the film, "Seven Years in Tibet," you have seen the strange custom displayed by the native inhabitants of that mountainous country at the sight of western, obviously foreign visitors. When the Tibetan people caught sight of the travelers, they stuck their tongues out at them, in a gesture that surprised the visitors.

However, this seems to be a universal trait, as it is manifested all around the world. In the West we have all experienced it as children when we used it as an act of defiance and rebellion, to eventually be promoted to clandestine self assertion status, when we are told that "It is not nice" by our mentors and parents, those large adults who assume authority and weild power over us. For who has not stuck their tongue out at a teacher or an adult when their back was turned, after having imposed their will upon us or scolded us about something or prohibited us from doing something we were intent on doing? When all grown up the gesture goes "underground" and we stick our tongue out mentally or emotionally, usually venting our suppressed feelings to others in a silent complaint or frustration.

Therefore it is a mark of defiance and no words are necessary. It is an immediate reaction to the behavior or radiation of another person or to their words or acts. It shows that we disagree, that we have a mind of our own, even if we are not allowed to express it or are told that it is not polite to do so.

So when the main character of "Seven Years in Tibet" responds to the native inhabitants of Tibet by mirroring their action, perhaps he is not being as respectful and cordial as he thinks.

The same gesture of sticking out their tongue was discovered in New Zealand when the first European travelers landed there. You have probably seen the custom in the film "Whale Rider."

Thus a universal gesture persists. From the standpoint of frequency, the tongue and saliva carry a person's radiation more intimately than, say, the hand. The saliva, being one of the body's liquids, carries a charge and by displaying one's tongue, one is projecting one's frequency faster and more effectively than with words. Thus by doing so a person asserts themselves and demonstrates their will, even if they are constrained and unable to act according to the dictates of their current feelings and compulsions.

Therefore, defiance, assertion and perhaps a touch of rebellion are demonstrated in a simple gesture that most of us in the West have quelled in ourselves because we have been told it was not nice, but nobody ever told us why.

The New Year

I am the New Year—here for a short twelve months only. A special new gift of time in twelve separate packages. As I arrive, everybody asks what I bring and what gifts will I reveal over the days and weeks to come. My reply to those who ask is simple: I come empty handed, ready and willing to assist. My gift is time and everything else must be won by those who want more. I will leave in twelve months to make room for my younger brother, next year, with my hands full of memories and experiences. But those will be the gifts that you bestow on me by your actions, thoughts and feelings.

Thus to those who pursue knowledge, knowledge shall be their companion or the lack of it shall be their spur; to those who desire riches—riches shall be their reward or the lack of them shall be their concern. For always the Law of Duality accompanies me and if you think you can escape the perennial manifestation of the duality of all things, you are wrong.

Thus, my advice to the human is this: learn to love the laws and live in harmony with the Mother, and it will follow that the laws will support your endeavors. If you don't live in harmony with the laws and expect only the good times, then you are denying yourself half of all available experiences and I can only become a disappointment to you as my days unravel, inevitably drawing to a close in December, when I will pass on the baton to my younger sibling, still unborn but already waiting in the wings.

So when you make your New Year resolutions, try to think beyond my tenure and take a glimpse into the rest of your life and consider what you want. Because only with long-term goals and aims will you be able to see clearly what you need to achieve this year, this month and today.

So I await your gifts, as I offer you mine—time to achieve what you really want and are prepared to pay for by your efforts and continuous application.

The Planet of Birds

If you were told that you were going to visit a planet run by intelligent birds, would you not expect a garden of paradise, a green and blue planet, full of nature reserves and running water?

If you then visited this planet and you were made welcome and decided to stay for a few days in one of their visitors' nests, wouldn't you find it surprising if you then found out that these birds had some strange customs? For example, if they tended to go to special salons to have their feathers dyed so that they may look prettier and younger, and even perhaps fool each other as to what specie of bird they hailed from or how old they were?

If you then found out that these birds lied, cheated, acquired so much bird seed and nest building materials that others had to go without, that they were driven by greed and polluted the very air they breathed and the water they drank, what would you think?

We expect birds to be natural; why do we not expect it of ourselves?

I look at my body and I am moved to address it, for the first time expressing my gratitude and appreciation in writing.

A Letter to My Body

I see you and you have served me well for over sixty years. Think—we have been together, sharing the same space for over half a century and it looks like you are still good for another decade or three!

Thank you for your service—ever faithful, ever trying. There were times when I did not treat you well, always expecting too much and thinking you woud last forever; there were times when I paid little attention to what I fed you with, both physically and electrically, and what demands I exerted upon you. However, miraculously you have survived the follies of my youth and through the years our partnership has improved. I listen to you now and I try to oblige your wants and needs, for I know that this is in both of our interests.

I wish to build a working relationship with you and will continue to try to be sensitive to your signals. Please communicate with me and I will be your willing student. For I know you have much to teach me, being that by heritage you are natural and aligned to the planet, domiciled here. I know I will not be taking you with me, wherever I go after death and that we shall part on that day. But until then, teach me please the ways and means of the planet, our Mother, and I will honor you both so that through you and Her I can find the way to the Father.
Thank you.

The Three Trains

I

General Habitual Living
(The known known)

These are two trains that pass through my station every day. One stops and I board it to go to work. It is a grey, dark, dull commuters' train, but it is reliable and familiar and it works like clockwork, according to schedule.

The other is an international express train and it does not stop at my station; in fact, it only stops at very few destinations. It zooms through, like a blue streak, brightly painted, with curtains at the windows and with a sleek, streamlined shape. I see blurs of faces in the windows looking out with curiosity, attempting to defy the speed and take in the sights of the countryside it is rushing through, looking out at local towns, the villages, the level crossings and the local people, like me.

To board this train I would have to travel to the town where it stops and I would have to be there at the right time. I would need to know its destination in order to buy a ticket. It would take me to new lands and I could sit at the window, looking out with curiosity and interest at the landscape, as it zooms by.

In the meantime, while I think about it and dream of foreign lands, I will board the local dingy train and go to work.

II

Initiative
(The known unknown)

I have decided to board the international express and take a holiday in a distant land. How exciting to travel for a few carefree days over mountains and valleys, crossing rivers and canyons, going through tunnels, cities, villages and towns. I see people board the train and disembark and as we travel, the languages change and I no longer understand what people are saying to each other. They shout and talk, they sell their wares at stations and the children wave to us as we ride past country roads and lanes. It is all so interesting and yet it does not last long, for soon the holiday is over and I must return.

On the way home the same route, the same scenery, the same languages and the changing faces and views do not seem so exciting any more, for everything reminds me that I am going back to my old familiar ways. While it lasted it was exciting and new and I thought it would change me forever. But now I am back in my own back yard and memories do not seem enough; I know I will soon start looking for my next adventure.

III

New Knowledge
(The unknown unknown)

Having taken the trip and returned I became dissatisfied with my everyday life and I began to search for more information and knowledge that would help me understand the purpose of my life. I was very lucky in my search and I found a wise old man who offered to help and explain about trains. I now know that although there have always been two trains that I could observe from my station, there are really three. The third is unseen and it is always there, ready for take-off. It can travel through the air, through space, through time, over mountains, valleys and seas. It is the magic train of the imagination and I don't need to go anywhere to climb aboard. All my faculties are here and ready for action. All I need to do is to let my imagination roam free, contemplating what is permanently real and true, rather than seeking for new thrills that never last. The truth lives within me and around me and in studying the workings of the body or discovering how, for example, a tree grows or why earthquakes happen, I am connecting to the natural worlds and slowly, in this quest for truth, I am discovering that I am part of a vast universe that is governed by a set of laws which is the same for all. I no longer will be bored, for if ever I am at a loss as to what to do next, I will board this third train of the imagination, driven by the human ability to think, compare, perceive and understand and I will go to the lands of awe and wonder (rather than wander), where all the unanswered questions of youth renew themselves in the fountain of the quest, bringing refreshed dwellings, musings, ponderings and meditations.

To be more specific — for example, in contemplating the phenomenon of spring, I begin to see the parallel between nature's ways and the ability of the human to renew themselves and give themselves a new chance and a fresh start. It all depends on attitude and the will to be and live and progress. This contemplation has found its expression in the following poem.

The Spring

Here I am again, your old friend, the spring
Why are you so surprised?
Every year you know I bring
Fresh color for your eyes.

Every year I reappear
Fresh and clean, brand new
Ready for renewal, I am near;
And now I ask—are you?

In the darkest winter hour
I do not stop and rest
I prepare my latent power
To do what I do best.

Every little rebirth
Offers me a stage
Every re-emergence
Opens up a page.
Each such effort I enhance
I will grow that which is true
I will come and do my dance.
And now I ask—will you?

The Fence's Lament

I am your fence — constructed to guard your property, to keep strangers out and protect those within. I am also a delineation to remind you and show the world which bit of the planet is temporarily "yours." Finally, I keep your possessions and activities away from pryng eyes so you can feel private, secure and isolated in your world.

I used to be part of a forest, growing high, up to the sky, alive and pulsating with sap and the nourishment of the planet. Now I am made to be uniform and precise, angular and pointed, rooted into the ground, but without roots.

I see and am participant in both sides — your world and the world outside and I do not see them as separate as you do, for to me the entire planet is integrated and one. So are you, if you could only see it. Despite your walls, your boundaries, borders, barriers, barbed wires, doors, fences, defences, gates, protections, securities, you share in the planetary life and are part of a large organization — the human race. Everything you do, no matter how many dividers protect you and isolate you, affects the whole, whether you like it or not.

And finally, no offence (no pun intended), but you also construct fences in your aura and then are surprised when others can't reach you and you are misunderstood. So realize that fences have become part of your world and so has possession and isolation. Know that this is not the natural way of the planet and I recommend you seek connections, rather than insulations, and see yourself as part of the organic life of the planet which is urging towards refinement and development as an organism in its entirety.

And one more thing — how can you possess the land

or space, when you are here as a visitor passing through in preparation for your onward journey? Does a traveler posess the waiting room at a railway station or the lounge at a busy airport? You can, however, leave your mark by helping to improve the place of your abode so as to give rather than take and share rather than hold.

This contemplation caused me to include here a translation of a poem by the Polish Romantic poet Cyprian Kamil Norwid:

> And even I own a small plot of land
> As large or small as a footstep indentation
> in the sand
> As long as I continue to walk forward.

Your Face

Humans do not see their face; perhaps they are not meant to. However hard you try, there is no way you can see your face direct—the eyes just will not come out on stalks and turn round to have a look, like a periscope; you cannot pull parts of your face far enough to lodge in front of your eyes. The only part of your face that you can possibly see is the end of your nose.

No doubt, someone will say that you can see your face in a mirror. Well, firstly, mirrors did not exist for hundreds of years and perhaps there is a reason for this. If God wanted us to have mirrors, we would be born with one. Secondly, the face we see in the mirror is not our real face but the one we put on for the moment of seeing our reflection—frontal approach, head straight, no frown, no excessive mimicry. The real reflection we mostly do not want to see. And the proof of this is in people's reactions when they see photographs taken of themselves when they didn't realize the camera was directed at them. They inevitably are surprised, hurt, disappointed and would prefer to tear the photograph up. There is also the moment when people are caught off-guard and see their reflection in, say, a mirror placed in a shop window, and suddenly, they straighten themselves up, pull their clothes into shape, try to look their best.

The fact that we can see ourselves in the millions of mirrors which exist in the world (how many do you have? Seriously — count them now) causes us to think about ourselves in a particular way — it influences our self view and makes us susceptible to advertising, fashion and general beliefs concerning the aesthetics of the day, such as, for example, the idea that old is ugly.

Perhaps we were not meant to see our faces in mirrors. We have been given permission to see other parts of our body without difficulty — we can see, appreciate and easily communicate with our hands, our legs, our feet, even our belly button, but not our face, where is lodged the only visible live part of the body — the windows to our soul, the most expressive part of ourselves, connected directly to the brain — the eyes. Perhaps God realized the self-induced pain we could be prone to putting ourselves through if we had to observe our own facial expressions every day, all day long. What would it be like, seeing ourselves on a continuous video or observing ourselves in a reflection, perpetually held in front of our eyes to see? Or what would it be like to permanently live in a dance studio with mirrors wall to wall?

God has given us a real mirror, in fact, many mirrors in which we can see the reflection of our face in a far more accurate, real and unbiased way. We continuously see ourselves in the reactions of other people around us. How they respond to us and what we do is the best possible mirror we could have and one that can offer encouragement, confirmation or correction. There is a continuous reading on how we are and how what we do turns up to others in their responses or lack of response, which changes and develops from day to day, according to how we change and move from depletion to well being, from happy to sad, from worry to joy—from mood to mood.

To judge the attractiveness of our face by how we see ourselves in the mirror could be a mistake, for our face is a working tool, a canvas on which our expressions, moods, emotions and thought processes appear. It is a forever changing "work in progress" and if there is something we don't like about it, it is easy to change—not through plastic surgery but through an energy process of altering the state that occurs behind and manifests through the eyes.

Aging

A ten-year-old looks at a 20-year-old and sees an adult who lives in a different world. A 20-year-old looks at a 30-year-old and sees someone who is definitely "past it" and "over the hill." A 30-year-old looks at a 40-year-old and sees someone past their prime, fixed, no longer young. A 40-year-old looks at a 50-year-old and sees someone who is slowing down and no longer up to very much. A 50-year-old looks at a 60-year-old and sees someone coming up to retirement, thinking of their remaining days and losing their ambition and zest for life. A 60-year-old looks at a 70-year-old and wonders what it is like to be at *death's door. A 70-year-old looks at an 80-year-old and wonders how they have managed to live so long. And yet, when we reach each of these ages ourselves, our perception changes.*

Age is clearly a matter of comparison and relativity. As we grow older, youth stretches like an elastic, extending into our increasing years, to encompass first 25, then 30 and even 35. Thus, as we get older, we see that there are more young people in the world. A 60-year-old might even call a 40-year-old parent of grown-up children "young." Hence the saying that policemen and doctors seem to grow younger all the time. As time moves on, it seems to go faster and faster, perhaps because there is so little of it left.

Between the ages of 10 and 20, 20 and 30, 30 and 40, 40 and 50, 50 and 60, 60 and 70, 70 and 80 we are given ten years to get used to the idea that yes, we will inevitably enter the next decade and that the next decade is valid too and in fact quite livable, providing we can find a way of thinking about being 30, 40 or 50 etc. There is time for values to shift; for example, during the 10 years between 30 and 40 the emphasis shifts from physical appearance and sexual performance (first self) to a growing concern with family, relationships, a career and/or religion (second and third self). As a person grows older, their values are meant to shift towards more permanent means of expression, otherwise they may become devastated by the deterioration of the physical temple (body) that houses the spirit, soul and electrical life.

Aging is a natural process and one of the enormous benefits of being older is that an older person knows and appreciates the feelings of a younger person, having been there themselves; a younger person can never know how someone older really feels. Within an older person there are many lives of all different ages and experiences which with development can be called upon at will and used to communicate with a representative of the younger generation.

If you have been to a place, you can picture it in your mind, imagine you are there and remember what it was like. If you haven't, you can only guess and work it out, but you can never really know for certain.

The 21st century western culture, in its worship of youth, has taken the dignity out of aging and the grace out of growing old. No one wants to be old any more; there is no honor in the fact of aging and the younger generations no longer cluster around to learn the wisdoms of the old, acquired on their journey of life. These times have introduced the retirement home, the old age pensioner's home, the senior citizens' apartment buildings, the retirement villages and golfing communities. The elders of the tribe used to be the wise ones, respected and listened to by all; nowadays they are kept out of sight and in isolation, unless they are fortunate enough to continue to work or to look after the next generation—the young children of the family. There is a natural affinity between the soon-to-depart grandparents who recognize and value the brightness of the newly arrived souls.

The astral light resists us, for it is full of insecurity and worry about getting old. It presses in on a person, even if they think they are settled to the age they are; for they may be settled now to being, for example, 40, but are they prepared for and settled to being 50, which is coming in 10 years' time?

The only way to survive the business of getting older is to acquire a larger view which sees the impermanence *of all things as part of Creation's plan. Can we therefore be different? We were not meant to stay the same age or live forever—we are on a journey from somewhere and are going somewhere, too. If we view this life as but a short sojourn and small part of our life in the universe, we can be glad of and interested in every stage of the journey, for each decade brings its own revelations and learnings and opens up new opportunities.*

To Think It Is to Create It
Or
Your Reality and You

I find it very strange that two people going through exactly the same experience can have two very different sensations, reactions, thought processes and results. This can turn up in such an extreme way that one will end up elated and the other depressed; one can be inspired and the other bewildered; one can be encouraged, while the other is disappointed. Thus it is not an external influence that shapes our lives, our health and moods, but how we think about what happens to us, how we shape our attitudes by our desires, expectations and knowledge.

One person can live in a self-induced hell inside their own head; to another life is an adventure and a purpose, no matter what anyone else around them thinks or says. It is for each person to design, build and cultivate the mental edifice of their choosing, within which they can proceed to live, settling in and unpacking their beliefs and thought processes into these self chosen surroundings. Thus one person might mentally live in a palace with many rooms, where each chamber is a new way of thinking and where revelation awaits; another might stubbornly proceed to inhabit only familiar rooms and walk along the same well-trodden paths, thinking the same thoughts for years or even decades.

There are enough thoughts in the world and universe for every single person to be totally original, fresh, new and excitingly innovative every single day of their life. The question is, how many people are daring enough to not give up the first time their expectations are not met or at the first sign of boredom or weariness?

Honesty
Towards a Fuller Understanding

This writing was inspired by the aspect of the Law of Duality that says that every thesis has its anti-thesis and that everything that exists, whether material or within the force realms, has its antidote, its nemesis or its opposite. This can be defined by the law of aerodynamics which says that every action has an equal and opposite reaction. Thus, if you move forward, the pressure of the air pushes against you; if you decide to do something, you immediately think of all the things that stand against it (or at least as many as your education and experience will allow). And if you do not think of them for yourself, you will certainly soon discover what they are by attempting to put into practice the initial idea or plan and if you do not encounter resistance yourself, others will no doubt educate you about the difficulties and obstacles you are facing in taking on a new initiative or project.

There are two ways to describe anything. The first is to focus on the thing itself and to describe its characteristics, attributes, shape, size, color, form; to describe its function, its purpose, its history, its action.

From this description an object will appear. However, the picture will be little related to its environment and will tend to stand on its own. The second way of describing something is to describe everything else, without hardly mentioning the object itself, thus creating a space or vacuum within which it can appear. Therefore, if I were to thus describe a car, for example, I could surround it with logistics, stories, anecdotes, without even mentioning the vehicle itself. I would talk about roads, the need for transportation, the progression of human culture through the Industrial Revolution, the invention of the steam engine and the mechanization of life, together with the advent of manufacturing plants, the development of factories, industries and the assembly line. Then there would be an assessment of the human need for travel and an evaluation of the need for speed and expediency. Having gone through all these aspects of human life in the 20th and 21st centuries, the picture of the car would very comfortably drop in the middle, for it would become clear that taking all the circumstantial evidence into account, the car could not not happen.

Another way to look at something is to try and bring together in one's mind the thesis and the anti-thesis, thus forming a better understanding of what the two, by their interaction and continuous 'rubbing' cause to exist. Take, as an example, a cup. You can describe a cup as a receptacle for liquid that is meant to be drunk from, made of clay or feïence or china or porcelain or plastic or paper. It has a flat bottom so that it can rest on flat surfaces and usually it has a handle so that it can be held without touching the surface which sometimes can be hot. The receptacle itself is usually round with walls that are not too wide so that they can be placed between the lips of the person who uses it. They come in all colors, shapes and sizes, but usually conform to the above basic description.

> DEFINITION ONE: *A cup is a receptacle for liquids for the purpose of drinking.*

Now, let us take a look at a cup from the standpoint of its anti-thesis. What is it not? It does not leak, it does not fall over, change shape, disintegrate, move around or spill. It is not difficult to hold, wash, pour into and out from. Clearly the first cup was made by someone who saw the need to bring an amount of water together so that a human could drink, rather than lick, slurp or use their hands to carry water from a stream or brook. Thus a cup is a bulwark against the nature of water, which tends to flow, move, disperse and trickle out of anything that is not waterproof. Water finds its own level and thus escapes from anything that is flat, has leaks or holes; it is quickly absorbed into any material that is porous, hygroscopic or has any form of air pockets within it.

> DEFINITION TWO: *A cup is a device to hold liquids into a unified shape for the convenience of drinking.*

This definition, as opposed to the first one, has a greater understanding behind it, for it takes into account both aspects of the Law of Duality: the thesis and the anti-thesis, in this case, the anti-thesis being the very nature of liquids.

Now, to move on a little further, from material examples to a more in-depth study of the nature of force, essences and power. Let's look at the word "honesty." Different people might have different ideas as to what honesty is, depending on their cultural background, education, morality and upbringing. In the study towards a better understanding, the attempt is to find a more objective way to discover the truth of something, rather than relying on one's perhaps limited training and experience. Thus, rather than considering honesty itself, let's have a look at what it is not. This is done because the definition of honesty could be deemed vague and controversial, evading clear-cut delineation. Its anti-thesis, however, is much more clearly defined and thus acceptable to anyone who has considered the matter. Thus, honesty clearly is not:

Dishonesty
Lies
Deception
Covering up
Hiding
Evasion
Avoidance
Fantasy
Embellishment
Unreality
Pretence
Airs and graces

Having now established a territory defining what honesty is not, by bringing the thesis (honesty) and anti-thesis together, it is much easier to see what honesty is. It begins to emerge, like in a darkroom photograph, slowly coming into focus. Thus, rather than defining the main object itself, we have also attempted to define the background against which it emerges into definition. Thus a new attempt at defining honesty could be:

> *DEFINITION ATTEMPT ONE:*
> *Honesty is a journey away from deception and*
> *unreality towards what is.*

From the above definition it becomes clear that honesty is not something that is cut and dried, definite, final and irrevocable. A new aspect of honesty has revealed itself in this deliberation and that is the sense of a journey and a target. Therefore honesty is an attempt to move away from lies, deception etc. into a territory where these antithetical essences have no entry. How can this territory be defined? There is only one word for it and that is the TRUTH. Thus,

> *DEFINITION ATTEMPT TWO:*
> *Honesty is a deliberate journey undertaken*
> *towards the truth.*

To arrive at the third attempt, let's take both aspects, already established: one, that honesty is a journey away from a set of essences describing possible human behavior; two, that this journey is towards the truth which is objective and stands on its own. Thus honesty has many stages, just as a train will stop at many stations as it journeys towards its destination. That is why honesty to different people will mean different things, depending on their development and understanding. However, the final destination or target is ultimate, final and irrevocable and can also be defined as WHAT IS. In bringing these two definitions together, we arrive at our third attempt:

> *DEFINITION THREE:*
> *Honesty is a journey towards the truth, with*
> *disregard for comfortability or self-preservation.*
> *Thus it has a non-personal quality of responding*
> *only to what is and not to what anyone might*
> *wish it to be.*

This process is itself a journey and thus it continues...

Mint Will Grow in the Garden

If you have ever planted mint in the garden, you will know that it grows in abundance and within a year or two it proliferates to such an extent that it takes over more and more territory, even dodging deliberately placed corrals and digging its way underneath other meticulously planted herbs and vegetables.

When finally you realize that it is beginning to thwart the rest of the garden growth, you decide to take action and clean up the garden, deliberately aiming at the offending mint. And no matter how many roots, spores, shoots and stems you pull out, no matter how big a pile of extinguished growth you carry to the compost heap, looking forward to next year's minty mulch, no matter how much effort you devote to eliminating the stubborn herb, you know deep down, instinctively and irrevocably, that mint will always grow in your garden.

This could be an analogy to describe many things, but I like to think of it as a parable for the human spirit. No matter how many difficulties befall a person, it will always rise up ready to try again. Our choice in the matter is not to stop it, but to support and propagate its indomitability to the point where we can learn to rely on its constant resurrective ability. In other words, we might not see how to overcome this obstacle or that setback, but our spirit does, for it cannot be vanquished or conquered as long as we live and breathe.

A Thought About Honor

Once something exists, its honor is in continuance. Thus maintenance and enhancement are its manifestation. For a baby this will appear as growth, feeding, discovery. There is a powerful honor from Creation to the human in providing the ways and means for maintenance. Thus, as we create, our honor is to provide continuance for that which we have created.

Everything wants to continue. Its honor is lodged within a thin thread that leads from its Creator that permits connection and feeding and maintenance. Thus honor is in the umbilical cord that Creation provides each time a new life appears.

Can we do less than maintain what we cause to exit?

Likes and Dislikes

It has been said that an illumined man or lady has very few likes and dislikes, for everything he or she does is aligned to purpose.

Do you like ice cream? And if you do, does that like control you or do you control it? And if you were told that ice cream was not good for you, would you still accept your like as part of your make-up and would you allow it to influence your going-on appetites?

Do you know what your likes are and do you manage them by giving them their time, their place and their space within your daily routine? Do your likes support your aims in life and your purpose, or are they incidental and unrelated? And if they pull you in the opposite direction to that in which you wish your life to progress, do you let them or do you try to squash them, ignore them, suppress them? Have you even thought about it and do you actually know what is the case? Have you sat down with a piece of paper and written down your likes and dislikes in all departments—physical, emotional, sexual, mental? Do you like a challenge? Do you like hard work? Because if you don't, you will probably not even consider your replies to these questions.

And what about dislikes? What do you dislike and why? Can you trace your dislikes to some past event, to a childhood trauma or another unpleasant period in your history? What about people? Who do you like and who do you dislike? Do you know why? If you don't, your likes and/or dislikes might be irrational. It really is worthwhile thinking about these issues—it is part of learning to know oneself and growing up to be a responsible, reasonable and sentient being. It is also part of the struggle to have one's mind rule one's emotions, rather than the other way round. Likes and dislikes are primarily governed by emotions and if a person allows emotions to rule, they can become unstable, unreasonable and even dangerous, both to themselves and others.

Your dislikes affect you even more than your likes, because these are the things (and people) that you will attempt to avoid at all cost. And what if you avoid what is good for you, what is progressive, healthy, challenging, educational, different, new—due to your programming?

In other words, do your dislikes stop you? Perhaps it is time to examine them, to take a closer look and to decide who and what you want to become, starting today, now...
Once that important decision is in place, have your likes and dislikes line up in support of that decision and serve you, together with your will haves and won't haves, almost like an army or police force that ensures the safety of your future chosen direction. Also, all your parts need to be informed of your wishes, otherwise they will not know how to help you. And the best way to help them help you is to inform them of your aims, by formulating them in a precise, clear and simple way, so that all your parts and you can understand and adhere to them.

These are a few thoughts concerning likes and dislikes that might help in the attempt to meditate upon the usefulness of one's desires. It is part of the process of sifting out what is important from what is not. After all, our time here on planet Earth is limited and why should we waste any of it on that which is not constructive or important?

Meditation About Likes and Dislikes

There are seven stages to this meditation process and each one is a step on a journey towards self-discovery and realignment.
The first stage introduces the idea that one's likes and dislikes are not necessarily the same as or even harmonious with the likes and dislikes of the body and faculties.
The second stage is to contemplate what you like that you do not yet know, or have not yet acknowledged.

Entities Yet Unknown

Oh entities yet unknown,
that call me from my future
I await your appearance and your wisdom
and your gifting;
You live in my next home
which is also your home
and I will meet you there
Where we will connect and talk and share.

I dare not think of what you are
or where you wait and dwell.
How can I? You are near and yet so far.
I cannot know what I don't yet know
And yet I know that I can grow,
to build a temple for you.

The new awaits, it beckons, calls
It's there, I know, beyond these walls.
The unknown is known, though not by name
It entices and challenges, never quite the same.
This now is now and I know it well
I can give it a word, a feeling, a spell
Tomorrow's now is unknown still
Tomorrow I will know it, describe it,
lend it my will.
Why can't I do so today?
Some things I may not yet know, others I may.

The third step in this meditation process is to do with finding the balance between inter-stimulation and sensation on the one hand and the suitability of likes and dislikes on the other.

It Has Been So Long...

It has been so long since living in harmony
with the Earth and the universe;
We need to learn how to be and what to do
Teach us oh Creation to discard our petty desires
And exchange them for yours.

When your needs are mine, I may become you
The human becomes the universe
The universe flows into the human
Both are one—God's children.
We have always been related,
Our path is joined if we let it be joint—
The search for a natural way.
Your laws are my law—I will abide by them,
No more trespassing into dark territories.
The light beckons, enlivens
and promises from our future.
As the crystal is a higher form than a rock
because its molecules are organized into a pattern,
So is the human who allows light to move through him
to illuminate what lies within.
To form a crystalline structure
to become transparent to the light,
Thus becoming one with the universe.
We are wanted. Do we want to want in return?

Stage four in this journey is to do with moving towards likes, as opposed to likes moving towards you.

What I Want

When what I want comes near,
The need for it will disappear.
As I integrate with my need,
It is the planting of a future seed.

Soon the two become the one
As the connection process is done.
Then I look for pastures new
In which to feel, to hear, to view.
What I want appears anew...

Stage five is an exploration of human life needs.

The Partnership

First I learn to listen to what my body says
I learn to respond to its needs.
Until its fulfillment becomes automatic
Then it will allow me my freedom to be and do
So that I can fetch higher food for it and for me.
Our future is in fulfilling both our potentials.
It becomes used and recycled;
I can move on to a higher destiny.
Magnify me, oh Lord.
It cannot be magnified,
But it can serve a magnification.
Its needs are never unreasonable.
Neither should mine be.

The sixth step is to do with declaring oneself to oneself within three realms, the first one of which is to do with well being and suitability; the second introduces the idea of adventurism and the third brings into focus the likes and dislikes of a person's living organism.

Out of the Dark

Out of the prison into the light—
Finding what charges and what feels right.
Every day something new, if only one thought
Never settling down to one's achieved lot.

Behind every hill is another hill still
Across every sea a new way to be
Beyond every mountain a new higher top
As long as I live it never will stop.

So on and on, life offers a test;
Move further along and promote the best.
As long as you move there is more room to grow
With every new learning there is more to know.

The man has not lived who has known it all
And life is too short to not answer the call.
Many responses can make a big sound,
Many small efforts can move the firm ground.

No matter how small, the chisel makes a mark
Even a tiny light will dispel the dark.
And after a while an image will appear
And attract other lights that will then draw near.

The final stage brings the entire process into a renewed focus with the consideration of durable value.

Meditation

Part One
Write down a number for each of the years you have been alive, starting with now and ending with one, to represent your first year. For example, if you are 25, you would write down 26 as your first number, representing the current year (still incomplete), all the way back to one. Starting from now (the current year), try to remember what had happened within each year and write down a word or a couple of words or a phrase to describe its trend (such as interesting, exciting, difficult, adventurous, change, full of initiative etc.).

Part Two
Write down each decade of your life separately: 0-10, 11-20, 21-30 etc. Try to find a phrase or expression for each age.

Part Three
Then look at your life as a whole and try to find the cycles and trends. If your life were a river, where would it be flowing to and how? Write down a few words to describe the journey so far, as if you were looking at the life of a stranger. What are the main characteristics of its flow?

Part Four
Make a decision about how you would want the flow of your life to continue and why.

Why Is the Human on Earth?

As a starter, here is an attempt to give ten answers to this question. It is recommended that you read the following after having attempted to answer the question yourself.

1. The human is the crowning resultant of Creation's creativity. It demonstrates Creation's urge towards the process of perfection, substituting one model for another until the best possible response can be guaranteed.

2. The human is an irritant, a piece of sand in an oyster, strategically placed where it can be catalytic and causative, engendering into its environment struggle, urge and persuasion towards the pearl of development.

3. The human houses the potential of Creation, being custodian to universal genes, preserved in safety for the future and toward a universal evolution and progression, waiting for the right circumstance and fermentation when they can be released into a new model.

4. The human is the produce of God, on a journey towards its Creator, shedding weaknesses as it progresses, becoming more and more like its final destination (or at least, that is the plan). The human has a universal job to do, to pollinate the universe into effective growth and refinement.

5. The human is a God ambassador, spreading codings into the lower reaches of the Ray of Creation, while at the same time learning about its temporary station and how not to be, in preparation for the next installment in its universal journey.

6. As a universal representative, the human is catalytic in causing a distillation of high essence from Creation, anchoring the plasma within which further evolution can happen.

7. Humans are on Earth as live incubators awaiting the population of the universe, once the planetary quarantine is lifted, due to human evolution and refinement.

8. Humans are on Earth to write their story, thus adding potency to the human astral light depository. As we humans have been given choice, this can move either way—towards evolution or away from it.

9. The human is the gatekeeper of the lower levels of Creation, guarding entrance to planetary level and being the decisive factor as to what can and cannot permanently anchor here.

10. Humans are here to learn and change state, in preparation for the next life to come.

11. The human is on Earth to process the unseen worlds so that they may find their expression and place, and grow in versatility and range.

Living with Grace

Why do people often destroy or lose the very thing they say they love? Why do they not appreciate their health until they lose it or are in danger of losing it? One could answer simply, "Because they are familiar with what they have," but there is more to understand about this trend in human behavior. For the question arises, why are we familiar with what we have? In observing human behavior, it becomes clear that inherent in the human design there is an urge and propulsion to learn, to explore, to grow. Let's, for the sake of argument, call this the green urge, because it is similar in nature to the urge of the grass and planetary vegetation, as it appears in the spring and is driven by an unseen power into expansion and fulfillment. Unless we humans override this natural urge, it is a powerful force within us and can be seen in each new generation of young children as they learn to walk, to speak and to become independent. They know not failure and giving up is not part of their mindset; they simply keep on trying again and again until they can stand on their own two feet and begin to move forward until they can pronounce individual words to their satisfaction, until they are ready to venture out on their own into the big world outside the safety of the family home where they grew up.

This urge pushes us all the days of our lives towards new learning, new understanding, new experiences, new businesses, new projects, increasing wealth, new relationships, new everything. Providing the basics are taken care of, our preoccupations move out of the realm of maintenance and into the realm of "what's next," which can lead to development or progression. Of course, there are those who manage to silent this urge, through the establishment of habitual responses, whether due to poor health, drug abuse, lack of education, a poor self-view, mourning or any other reason that can spin a person away from the natural inbuilt curiosity and need for progress. Sometimes the pursuit of something new can become a threat to a person's well being and continuance. But when the green urge is there, it continuously takes a person another step away from the familiar and beyond the established, the already accomplished, the status quo, and therefore it will lead them away from their maintenance life into realms of initiative, where the unknown hides in the shadows.

Take, as an example, a person who becomes employed in a new job. At first everything is interesting and new, and even finding one's way to the coffee machine in the morning can be a challenge. Then there is the need to learn everyone's names, to understand the filing system and to get inside the computer programs. Then, once a routine has been established and our employee begins to fit comfortably into the ways and means of the office staff, the familiar urge sets in, unless, of course, a person is settled to be part of a routine or finds ways to advance with the job or the job itself offers a continuing challenge. Otherwise they will soon start looking around for better, more interesting employment and higher remuneration. What was once a gratefully received position, full of promise and challenge, becomes boring and routine.

So how can one safeguard against compromising what has already been achieved, to make sure that with each new adventure one does not jeopardize what one has already achieved? Well, there are no guarantees, but if one can find ways to avoid familiarity, then perhaps one will value what is already in place enough to not destroy it or neglect it every time something new and stimulating turns up. There are so many stories of people losing everything in their pursuit of assumed happiness that perhaps we can take their hard earned lessons as a warning that what we do have is very valuable, and a platform for what we are about to set out to achieve. Let us not forget the one bird in the hand, be it our home, our health, our relationships or simply the fact that once again we are able to put food on our table for one more day, before we go chasing those other birds in the bushes. An appropriate appreciation for what is already in place will provide the strength and security to venture safely into new territories, thus satisfying the green urge as well as promulgating grace as a way of life.

The Trail of Tears

The Cherokee native American tribe that used to live in Tennessee were forcibly removed from their lands back in 1838 when they were marched for over 1,000 miles all the way to Oklahoma. This tragic event became known as the Trail of Tears. The journey, during which 4,000 people died of exhaustion and disease, began on the bank the Tennessee river at a place that is called Blythe Ferry. When considering the tragic story of the native tribes of North America, I have often wondered what mark could be made in the astral light to help heal the hurt and sorrow of so many years at the hand of the white man.

On the spot where the infamous journey began there is currently a Cherokee Removal Park and a monument will be built on the escarpment to mark the place and time in history. The park is isolated and not easy to find; it lies on the migration route of eagles, herons and many other birds. An ideal place for meditation and a quiet ceremony, dedicated to the memory of those thousands of people who suffered in the past.

The Trail of Tears

Standing on the shore of the Tennessee
Looking into the future, but it's hard to see
Trying to peer into the coming months and years
Everything that appears is through a veil of tears.
Ten thousand people are standing next to me
A great human river as far as the eye can see
Ferried across the grey Tennessee
To some other place they don't want to be.
I swear to remember the freedom we once knew
For our story of the many must be told by the few.

After a brief rest the militia are urging us on
What keeps us alive is the drum and the song.
Four thousand perish and die on the way
Never to see the dawn of another new day.
Goodbye to the Smokys and memories of old
For we will return to our ancestors' fold.

The Wand of Youth and the Dawn of Life

Enter a life—keen and eager, willing to learn with an urge to know more, to be able to do. Then the young human struggles for independence and release from parental constriction. Once having achieved it, he or she often wishes someone or something would take care of them.

In our early years everything is done for us and we do not have to worry about anything. Decisions are made for us and our first independent stance manifests itself when we want to begin to make our own decisions about what we wear, what we eat, what we do and how we do it, if only to make a statement that the time has come to assert ourselves, to strike out on our own and begin to make our own individual mark.

We are full of energy and well being, ready to try almost anything, hungry for experience, knowledge and sophistication. The world is a very big place, full of mystery and wonder and the years stretching ahead of us seem long and almost endless. In our minds we are immortal, ready for conquest.

The mystery of life begins and we know not what lies ahead. So much seems possible and we look around for areas to get into, subjects to study, jobs to fulfill. The slow process of specialization begins and people around us begin to define our talents for us and suggest career paths or possible profitable territories within which we can win. Every new choice is also a limitation, as we make our decisions and taking something up, we put other things down. Our personal evolution begins and within it we develop some talents, whilst others lay dormant and unused. No one can be everything or take up versatility as a way of life, and yet the story of the Renaissance man is a true one and if this is the time of rebirth, then perhaps a new possibility and permission to pursue the truth of all things is presenting itself, within the framework of an enhanced faculty.

Perhaps the world is growing young again and for those who can feel, register and connect to this new potency there will be no need to shut oneself off from the many wonders presented therein. Perception will be possible on several levels all at once so that no human will have to limit themselves to one path, one way, one career, one specialization, one philosophy, one religion.

As the playwright Terentius wrote, "Homo sum; humani nil a me alienum puto" (I am a human being, so nothing human is strange to me).

When I Die...

When I die—you will see me passing by
A look, a gesture, a wink of an eye—
I will be a migrating bird, high up in the sky
I will companion you when I die.

The immortal times we had and shared
Are witness to the warmth and care
The live endearment we have had,
The times of being happy, sad.

So when we're gone and passed away
These holy substances will stay
To find a new stage on which to play
And gift another with a better day.

June 30th, 2002

When I Die 2...

When I die there will be no more pain
No questions, no answers, no need to explain
Unless reincarnation means I will come back again—
When I die there will be no more pain.

Streets of the Mind

Streets of the Mind

All these writings are about words, which end with the letters "st" — thus streets. Some are to do with the level of superlatives, i.e. "most, best, etc." which most humans aim for. The rest are simply words ending in "st."

Boa Street

I live on Boa Street. Indeed it is a constricting place to be and live. Everyone knows everything about everybody and nobody believes a word of it.

As you try and represent yourself in the best light possible, mentioning only the good things that happen to you and the many excellent qualities and talents you possess, so is everyone else attempting to do the same. Thus there is a lot of competition on Boa Street, with people shouting their own praises and demonstrating their virtues.

And everyone longs for a little bit of quiet because deep down they know that real quality can be felt and needs no advertisement.

Lo Street

Don't go down Lo Street, or you might never come back! Easy to say, but we all end up going there at some time or other. How do we know we are there? We don't, and even if others tell us we are, we tend not to listen. It is only in hindsight that you can see you have been to Lo Street.

If you actually know for certain that you are on Lo Street, then you have already taken a step away from it and are no longer there.

Co Street

Those who walk down Co Street need to pay for the privilege. Nothing is free here, nothing is unearned. But because of this, there is value for everything and nothing is wasted. Even the words you use have to be paid for here and everyone is very careful and deliberate about what they say, how they say it and how long it takes them to say it. The very air you breathe here has a price tag attached to it too and everyone breathes fully and deeply, making sure they make the best usage of that irreplaceable nutriment.

The street is clean and everything has its place, for even the steps you take are paid for. And as each moment passes on Co Street, it moves from the still available account to the already used aggregate. Today's payment becomes yesterday's history and the story of one's life accumulates to itself wealth and dividends or debt and extra payments, depending on how fully each moment is used up and appreciated. Depending on how a person uses their time within their time, so will they be paid back when they run out of time.

Pa Street

I often walk down Pa Street and look into the store windows, peer over the walls and fences of gardens and sneak a view of doorways, as I pass by. Every day I add a brick to the construction of Pa Street as I get older; and so it increases in variety and changes all the time with each new addition.

Some parts I hardly visit at all, others I wish to forget. As I walk down the street again, I try to look anew, not so much at each nook and cranny, but at the style and trends of the architecture, the way the street itself is paved and the countenance of the people I meet therein. Above all I wonder, where is this street leading to? And what will it look like when it is complete and finished?

La Street

To some there is a sense of desperation down La Street and two very distinct and different types of people pound its sidewalks — those who wish they could stay but are moving out, for whatever reason, or those who deliberately have decided to move out and are glad to do so.

And then there is a third category of people who attempt to make the finality of life on La Street into a longevity; for them it is a continuance, for as long as they are able to make the last moment last. Theirs is the value for the gift of each passing second and the longing for it never to end; they live their lives with the attitude that always it is a good day to die.

Mo and Be Street

Mirror, mirror on the wall — who is the most beautiful of all? The most skilled, the wisest, the best? Why is the Guiness Book of Records the most popular book in the world? Why are the Olympic Games the most popular international events with millions of people watching every discipline on TV, beamed by satellite to hundreds of countries the world over? We seem to need to know the limits of our own possibility so that we can look to those who are breaking new ground and thus relinquish our own opportunity. Or perhaps, when approaching the vast fields of new, un-chartered territories, we can withdraw into safety and wait for the record breakers and trend setters to venture therein.

Isn't it surprising how no matter how great a record, how huge the effort, there will always be someone who breaks it in the end? Every year there are new records in most disciplines, as the human bar is raised higher and higher by the invisible hand of competition and ambition. If we had no one to measure ourselves against, how far or how high would we go?

If we never knew who the best, the most, the fastest were, perhaps in our minds we would never set the limits of our own capability and, like the Rumanian gymnasts who were never introduced to the idea of world records and setting limitations to their abilities, we would soon soar above the magnetic pull of our own history and our self-manufactured view of what we can and cannot be and become.

Fa Street

People are always rushing on Fa Street, and then they say with surprise, "Doesn't life pass by quickly?" On Fa Street people do get older quicker and they somehow never have the time to fit in a day everything they would want to do.

Fa Street is full of fast food restaurants, "same day" and "while-you-wait" services. No one wants to wait for a doctor, a dentist or a take-away, so all waiting rooms are banned. The books are thin and contain mostly pictures and even the movies are short. People rush by as you walk down Fa Street with no time to look you in the eye or say good morning... There is not much time for a smile or a laugh on Fa Street, and holidays are short and cut back to a minimum.

There are special policemen on Fa Street making sure you do not smell the flowers on the way.

Be careful, if you go to live on Fa Street, because life itself just might pass you by without you even noticing how or when it had happened.